# Raw Food Diet
## Cookbook
### For

# Vegans, Fruitarians and Vegetarians

## Over 500 New and delicious 100% Raw recipes

### By

# Christina Hills

# Introduction

A raw food diet is that which involves mainly unprocessed, whole, plant-based, and preferably organic, foods. Three-quarters of the person's diet should consist of uncooked food.

Typically, about 70 percent or more of the diet consists of raw food. Staples of the raw food diet are fruits, vegetables, sea vegetables, nuts, seeds, sprouted grains, and beans. Gently heating food is considered acceptable, as long as the temperature doesn't go above 118 degrees Fahrenheit. While most people who are on a raw food diet plan are vegan, some eat raw animal products, like raw milk, cheese made from raw milk, or raw fish or meat.

This cookbook helps you enjoy a clean, Plant-based, healthful approach to eating that will transform your health by eating Vegetables, Fruit, Nut and seeds. Whether you are switching up a few weeknight meals or completing overhauling your diet, this cookbook walks you through the essentials of raw diet

- **Breakdown of the Raw Food Diet for beginners:** This cookbook starts with a thorough breakdown of the diet for newbies by defining the diet itself, the benefits, food to eat and those to avoid, tips on how to introduce the diet into an existing diet and ways to get all desired nutrient from the diet.
- **Raw Food Recipes**: Over 500 recipes that are categorized into Dessert, Breakfast, Main Dishes, Soup and Side, Salad & Dressing
- **Raw Food Substitutions**: Refer nut-free options plus substitution tips swap ingredients

# Stuffed Avocados with Crunchy Asian Cabbage Slaw

**Hands-On Time: 20 Mins || Total Time: 20 Mins**

**Category: Breakfast**

**Yields: 4 servings**

## Ingredients

- 1 cup shredded red cabbage (I recommend using a mandolin)
- 1 cup shredded green cabbage
- 3/4 cup grated carrot (about 1 carrot)
- 1/2 cup shaved red onion
- 4 green onions, thinly sliced
- 1 Tbsp minced fresh ginger
- juice of 1 lime
- 2 Tbsp mirin
- 1 Tbsp rice vinegar
- 1 Tbsp turbinado or brown sugar
- 2 tsp toasted sesame oil
- 2 avocados, halved and pitted
- sesame seeds

## Instructions

1. In a medium bowl, mix together both cabbages, the carrot, red onion, and green onion.
2. In a small bowl, whisk together the ginger, lime juice, mirin, rice vinegar, sugar, and sesame oil. Pour over the cabbage mixture and toss to combine.
3. Carefully scoop a hole in each avocado half. Fill with the slaw and top with sesame seeds. Enjoy!

NOTES

For a smaller appetizer version, top a rice cracker or sesame cracker with a small slice of avocado and a spoonful of slaw. Garnish with sesame seeds.

# Raw Granola with Edible Blossoms

**Prep Time: 10 min || Total Time: 10 min**

**Cuisine: Vegan**

**Makes: 3-4 servings**

## Ingredients

- 4 cups Whole Oats, Soaked overnight or at least 4 hours
- ¾ cup Raw Almonds (I used honey-glazed almonds), chopped
- ¾ cup Raw Walnuts, chopped
- ½ cup Raw Sunflower Seeds
- ¼ cup Raw Pecans, chopped small
- ½ cup Raw Honey (Know your farmer if possible, mine's from a family member in Oregon)
- ¼ cup Agave or Maple (very optional)
- 1 Tbs Cinnamon (or to taste)
- 1 tsp Pink Himalayan Salt

## Directions:

1. Gently blend all ingredients together in a big bowl.
2. Spread on to dehydrator sheets (I didn't use parchment and nothing dripped through).
3. Dry until crunchy/crispy
4. Take out and add more honey and cinnamon to taste, put back in dehydrator until crunchy and done!

5.  I added some edible blossoms from my yard (lavender petals, Bok Choy blossoms, borage, pansies and violas).  You can always add in dried fruit, more nuts, seeds, spices, anything you like.
6.  Top with homemade nut milk, I used hemp milk but all taste good.
7.  Enjoy & Keep Eating Your Plants!

# Strawberry Caramel Tarts

**Prep Time: 10 min || Total Time: 10 min**

**Cuisine: Vegan**

**Makes 3-4 servings**

Raw Recipe Crust

- 1 cup shredded coconut
- ½ cup pecans
- 1 cup walnuts
- 6 Medjool dates (or 12 soaked normal dates)
- 2 tablespoons Agave Syrup
- ¼ teaspoon salt
- 2 tablespoons melted Coconut Oil

Raw Recipe Caramel

- 2 cups of soaked dates – soak for two hours minimum, then drain
- ¼ cup Raw Honey
- 1 tablespoon Almond Butter (you can omit if you can't find it or can't find a raw version. Add 1 more tablespoon of honey instead)
- 2 tablespoons Almond Milk
- ¼ teaspoon salt

Raw Recipe Strawberry Topping

- 500g fresh washed and quartered or halved strawberries
- 2 tablespoons Agave Syrup

## Instructions

1. Soak dates for caramel and base prior to making the raw receipt with suggested times.
2. To make the Raw Crust, combine the nuts in the food processor and blend until finely chopped. Add the rest of the ingredients and blend until a doughy, chunky mix is formed.
3. Press into greased tart tins or you can use muffin tins, or a large cake tin to make one large tart/flan.
4. Cool for 4 hours in the freezer to set prior to filling. DO NOT MISS THIS STEP!
5. Combine all caramel ingredients in a food processor and process until really smooth.
6. Pour into tins, moulds or whatever you are using. Gently lay all strawberries into your circular layers and add the whole strawberry in the middle for presentation.
7. To get your Agave Syrup really runny, place in a bowl in the sink with warm water about 20 minutes prior to use. Gently pour a dash of agave syrup over each one to get the strawberries shining. Chill for 3 – 6 hrs and then serve.

# Amy's Pea and Cucumber Dip/Spread

## Prepare your sprouted peas

- 1/2 cup dried peas

## Instructions

1. Soak overnight in 1 cup water, rinse and drain in the morning and put in a tub in a cupboard.
2. Repeat this the next two days. They should now have little tails.

To the peas add;

- 2-3" diced cucumber
- 1 tsp nutritional yeast
- A couple of fresh sage leaves or some mint
- 2 cloves of garlic
- 1-2 tbsps olive oil

## Instructions

1. Puree with a hand blender if available or a liquidizer (in this case put cucumber and oil in first)
2. Season with salt and freshly ground black pepper

# Raw Salted Blueberry Chocolate Tart

**Recipe type: Dessert**

**Cuisine: raw vegan**

## Ingredients

For The Crust:

- 70 grams hazelnut flour
- 75 grams almond flour
- 2 tablespoons coconut oil
- 2 tablespoons maple syrup
- pinch sea salt

For The Filling:

- 1.5 cups dates, soaked overnight and drained
- ¼ cup cashews
- ¼ cup warm water
- seeds of ½ fresh vanilla bean
- 80 grams 70% dark chocolate, melted

For The Topping:

- 1 cup fresh blueberries
- 30 grams chocolate, melted
- ½ tsp coconut oil or ghee
- ½ teaspoon coarse sea salt k

**Instructions**

1. In a Cuisinart or blender, combine hazelnut flour, almond flour, coconut oil, maple syrup, and sea salt.
2. Blend to combine.
3. Remove dough from your blender and form into a ball.
4. Press evenly into a tart pan (mine is irregular at 8 inches wide, but you could use two 4.5-inch-wide tart pans).
5. In a blender, combine drained dates, cashews, warm water, vanilla bean, and melted chocolate and blend until creamy in consistency (it took me about 1 minute, total, stopping to scrape down the sides every 15 seconds or so).
6. Spoon out filling over your raw crust.
7. Spread evenly.
8. Top with blueberries, in no particular arrangement.
9. Combine last of the chocolate with coconut oil or ghee, stirring to thoroughly combine.
10. Using a small spoonful at a time, spoon melted chocolate over your berry topping (I used two spoonfuls).
11. Sprinkle coarse salt over.
12. Serve chilled.

# Table of Content

# RAW FOOD DIET

The raw food diet has roots as far back as the late 1800s, when a doctor believed he cured his own case of jaundice by eating raw apples. Since then, the diet has evolved into its current form, and has waxed and waned in popularity. Sometimes people shift from a vegetarian diet to a vegan one and then to a raw one.

A raw food diet involves mainly unprocessed, whole, plant-based, and preferably organic, foods. Three-quarters of the person's diet should consist of uncooked food.

Typically, about 70 percent or more of the diet consists of raw food. Staples of the raw food diet are fruits, vegetables, sea vegetables, nuts, seeds, sprouted grains, and beans. Gently heating food is considered acceptable, as long as the temperature doesn't go above 118 degrees Fahrenheit. While most people who are on a raw food diet plan are vegan, some eat raw animal products, like raw milk, cheese made from raw milk, or raw fish or meat.

Eating a raw food diet means consuming fresh, nutrient-rich plant foods that have not been heat processed. When foods are cooked, much of their important disease-preventing nutrients are lost.

Conversely, a raw diet provides you with a greater degree of health and vitality, slows aging, and promotes healing. By making the majority of your diet healthy raw foods and avoiding unhealthy alternatives, you can improve your health and reduce your risks of suffering from a degenerative disease. Getting started with this nutritious lifestyle is easy.

Raw food dieters believe that eating a high proportion of raw foods makes them healthier. Some raw foodists are vegan, and they consume no foods of animal origin. Others eat raw meat and raw animal products.

# What can I eat in Raw Diet?

Some foods, like fresh fruits and vegetables, are easy to identify as raw. Other ingredients, such as nut butters, agave nectar, almond milk, olive oil, soy sauce, and cocoa, aren't always raw, so you may need to read labels and take time to find brands that pass muster.

Foods that have the words roasted, dry-roasted, toasted, cooked, or baked on the label are not raw. Neither are canned foods.

## Compliant Foods

- Whole, unprocessed foods
- Organic fruits, vegetables, and nuts
- Sprouted or germinated beans and grains
- Recipes prepared from raw ingredients

## Vegetables

Use vegetables in salads, smoothies, blended dressings, and soups. Vegetables can also be pickled or made into noodles. Frozen vegetables that have been blanched or boiled before being frozen are not considered raw.

Also look for sea vegetables, such as arame, dulse, kelp, wakami, and unroasted nori sheets.

## Fruits

Fruits can be whole, dried, dehydrated, or used in juices or smoothies. Frozen fruit is considered raw. Superfoods such as raw cacao powder, cacao nibs, carob powder, and goji berries are all permitted on a raw food diet.

## Nuts and Seeds

Look for raw and preferably organic nuts and seeds. Use them in smoothies, pesto, butters, non-dairy milk, cheeses, gravy, cream, and ice cream. You can also use a dehydrator to make raw chia or flax seed crackers.

## Grains

Whole grains, such as millet, buckwheat groats, kamut, quinoa, oats, wheat germ, spelt, and wild rice are all permitted on the raw food diet, but will need to be germinated or sprouted.

## Beans and Legumes

Some raw beans (such as chickpeas, adzuki beans, mung beans, and lentils) can be eaten after they have been soaked and sprouted, but others, such as kidney, soy, and fava beans, are considered unsafe to eat.

## Fats

Raw sources of fat include avocados; raw coconut oil and butter; cold-pressed, extra-virgin olive oil; chia oil; raw flaxseed oil; and raw hemp seed oil.

## Beverages

Aside from purified water, raw foodists drink barley grass juice, vegetable or fruit juice (freshly squeezed or frozen, unpasteurized), young coconut water, and wheatgrass juice. Caffeine is not permitted, so black and green tea and coffee are excluded from the diet. Herbal tea (even if it's made with water heated to less than 118 F) isn't considered raw because the leaves are usually heated during the manufacturing process.

## Fermented Foods

Foods produced by fermentation are permitted on the raw food diet. These could include coconut kefir and yogurt, kimchi, miso paste, and sauerkraut.

## Herbs, Spices, and Condiments

While table salt is not permitted on the raw food diet, Himalayan salt and Celtic sea salt is allowed, along with other seasonings:

- Apple cider vinegar

- Basil
- Bragg's Liquid Aminos
- Cayenne
- Chives
- Chocolate, raw
- Cinnamon, ground
- Cumin, ground or seeds
- Curries
- Dill
- Ginger root
- Nama shoyu (raw soy sauce)
- Parsley
- Vanilla beans, raw
- Vinegars

## Sweeteners

Most sweeteners are processed and not truly raw, but the following are permitted: raw agave nectar, coconut nectar, raw honey, mesquite powder, stevia powder, date sugar, and yacon syrup.

# Foods to avoid on Raw Diet

Different people have different interpretations of the raw food diet and what it means. Some people will eat some cooked food, while others eat none. For some people, it is a way of life. For others, it is simply a dietary choice.

- Non-Compliant Foods
- Foods heated above 118 degrees F
- Refined, processed, or pasteurized foods
- Foods treated with pesticides
- Caffeine
- **Olives:** They are bitter if eaten raw. However, a raw foodist can eat olives if they are raw and sun-cured. Salt preserves most olives, and olives in cans are often cooked.
- Table salt
- Coffee, tea, and alcohol
- Pasta

# Preparing the food

- A raw foodist prepares food in a special way.
- The only heating that is allowed is with a dehydrator. This blows hot air through the food. The temperature is never above 116 Fahrenheit, or 46 degrees Celsius. Raw foodists also may also blend and chop up their foods.
- Grain and bean seeds are eaten soaked and sprouted rather than whole
- Nuts can be soaked, and some fruits are dried
- Many fruits and vegetables are juiced or used in smoothies

### Soaking and Sprouting

Raw beans, legumes, nuts, and seeds contain enzyme inhibitors that are normally destroyed with cooking. The nutrients can be released by soaking them (germination) or sprouting them.

Germination involves soaking in water for a specific amount of time. Although the recommended germination times vary from two hours (for cashews) up to one day, some raw foodists say that soaking overnight is sufficient and more convenient. It's important to start with dried, raw, preferably organic seeds, beans, legumes, or nuts.

Rinse beans, nuts, legumes, or seeds and place in a glass container. Add room temperature, purified water to cover. Soak at room temperature overnight (mung beans require a full 24 hours). Rinse a couple of times prior to use.

After germination, seeds, beans, and legumes can be sprouted. After they are drained during the final step of the germination process, place them in a container for sprouting. Leave them at room temperature. The seed, bean, or legume will open and a sprout will grow from it. Rinse the sprouted nuts or seeds and drain well. They can be stored in an airtight container in the refrigerator for up to five days.

## Dehydrating

Foods can be gently heated using a piece of equipment called a dehydrator to simulate sun-drying. Dehydrators are enclosed containers with heating elements that warm food at low temperatures. A fan inside the dehydrator blows the warm air across the food, which is spread out on trays. Dehydrators can be used to make raisins, sun-dried tomatoes, kale chips, crackers, breads, croutons, and fruit leathers.

## Blending and Juicing

Foods can be blended or chopped using a food processor or blender to make smoothies, pesto, soup, and hummus. Vegetables and fruit can also be juiced.

## Fermenting

Fermented foods include sauerkraut, raw coconut yogurt, raw macadamia nut cheese, and kimchi.

## Modifications

A raw food diet is compatible with vegetarian, vegan, and gluten-free diets.

Cooking protects from food-borne illnesses (such as E.coli).

**PS: A raw food diet isn't recommended for pregnant women, children, older adults, people with weak immune systems, and those with medical conditions.**

People with a history of eating disorders or those who are underweight should consult their healthcare provider before trying the raw food diet, because it tends to be very low in calories.2

# Benefits of Raw Diet

Raw fruit contains a wealth of vitamins that protect the body from harmful free radicals. These free radicals contribute to chronic diseases like cancer and heart disease.

If you worry about stuffing yourself with carbohydrates when you eat fruit, remember that fruit is a simple carbohydrate, and the sugars are easily absorbed by cells as a fuel source.

Since you're consuming whole fruit, you're also getting fiber and high doses of antioxidants. While protein should definitely be the star of your breakfast, you'll want to include a healthy dose of fruit and chopped nuts and seeds for healthy fats as well.

Vegetables provide high amounts of minerals like iron, calcium, and magnesium that our bodies need for metabolic processes, nerve function, and a whole host of other important tasks.

It's a balance of different minerals that helps the body maintain normal health. Of course vegetables also contain lots of antioxidants, so you'll want to include lots of fruits and vegetables in your raw food diet.

1. Raw foodists claim that consuming mainly uncooked foods can lead to weight loss.
2. Cutting out processed food means many new raw food dieters will probably lose weight at first.
3. They also believe that with a raw food diet, the body is better able to prevent and fight diseases, especially chronic diseases.
4. Some nutrients, for example, water-soluble vitamins B and C, are reduced or destroyed by cooking, so eating food raw ensures a better supply of these.
5. This, they say, is because raw and living foods contain essential food enzymes. Heating the food to above 116 degrees Fahrenheit, or 47 degrees Celsius, destroys these food enzymes.
6. Raw foodists maintain that enzymes are the life force of a food. Nature has given each food its unique perfect mix. These vital enzymes allow us to fully digest our foods without having to rely on our own digestive enzymes.
7. Raw food dieters argue that the cooking process destroys or alters these enzymes, as well as essential vitamins and minerals. Only raw food, they say, is "live" food.
8. Cooked foods, they say, take longer to digest, and they clog up the digestive system and arteries with partially digested fats, proteins, and carbohydrates.

Raw food dieters maintain that a person on the diet will experience:

- More energy
- Clearer skin
- Better digestion
- Weight loss
- Lower risk of developing heart and cardiovascular disease
- Reduction in risk of cardiovascular disease, cancer, obesity, and type 2 diabetes.

# Raw Food Staples to Keep on Hand

With a bit of planning and preparation, you can enjoy the health benefits and culinary rewards of raw food any time. To make mealtime a snap, here's a list of raw foods to keep stocked:

- Versatile fruits such as blueberries, oranges, bananas, and avocados
- Fresh, in-season vegetables
- Leafy greens, including kale, spinach, cabbage, and romaine lettuce
- Soaked raw nuts and seeds
- Sprouted or steamed gluten-free grains such as quinoa, millet, and buckwheat
- Sprouted or cooked legumes, including lentils, peas, chickpeas, and beans
- Probiotic-rich foods such as raw sauerkraut, miso, and raw yogurt

# Getting Proper Nutrition on a Raw Food Diet

When you start transitioning to a raw food diet, knowing what to eat can be tough. Be adventurous and try new things, but also be sure to follow these eating tips to ensure you get proper nutrition:

- Eat a wide variety of fresh, ripe, raw, organic fruits and vegetables.
- Consume all the colors of the rainbow to get a full spectrum of nutrients.
- Make nutrient powerhouse green foods the largest portion of your diet.
- Consume a variety of raw nuts and seeds in moderation.
- Include foods that are rich in omega-3 fatty acids.
- Minimize fried foods, saturated fats, and oils.
- Soak and sprout nuts, seeds, and legumes before eating them.
- Choose organic whenever possible to minimize chemical residues.
- Minimize or eliminate meat and dairy products from your diet.
- Reduce sweets and concentrated sweeteners, like white sugar, corn syrup, evaporated cane sugar, and sugary drinks such as soda, candy, and desserts made with sugar.
- Use only a moderate amount of salt.
- Choose gluten-free grains such as quinoa, millet, amaranth, and buckwheat.
- Supplement with vitamin B12.
- Supplement with vitamin D if you aren't getting enough sunshine.

# Surprising Natural Foods to Avoid on a Raw Food Diet

When you hear the words raw food diet, you probably correctly assume that it doesn't include fried, roasted, baked, or grilled foods. You may also realize that most raw foodists avoid highly processed, sugary, salty, and oily foods. But that's not the whole story.

Here are a few more foods that may appear healthy at first glance but don't measure up to raw standards:

- **Roasted nuts and seeds**: Select raw varieties of seeds and nuts to avoid free-radical damage to your cells. Soak these foods before eating them to enjoy maximum nutrition.
- **Soy foods:** Common allergens often hidden in prepared foods like veggie burgers and soy meat analogs (fake meat) can be replaced in burgers and meat substitutes using soaked nuts, mushrooms, and root vegetables.
- **Wheat (except wheat grass), breads, pastries, pastas, and "wheat meats" (seitan)**: Use sprouted grains, soaked nuts, and vegetables such as zucchini to make breads, crackers, and even pasta.
- **Vinegar:** Use citrus juice and other acid fruits in dressings, marinades, and sauces in place of vinegar, which can cause digestive problems.
- **Honey:** Using agave nectar, date paste, or coconut syrup is a better option for small children and others with immune system challenges.
- **Refined sugar:** Use dates or other dried fruit, agave nectar, coconut sugar, or stevia instead to keep your blood sugar at healthier levels.
- **Iodized salt:** Use Himalayan crystal salt and avoid chemical additives.

# Keeping to Raw Foods when Traveling and Socializing

Maintaining a raw lifestyle away from home may seem daunting at first. By planning ahead and packing some of your own ingredients to enhance the raw offerings available at your destination, you can ensure that you have a healthy and satisfying meal just about anywhere. Pack these items when you're eating raw on the road, at a friend's, or at other away-from-home places:

- Avocados
- Raw seeds and nuts
- Raw bread, flax crackers, or croutons

- Kale chips
- Favorite herbs and spices
- Nori sheets
- Vegetarian-formula nutritional yeast
- Himalayan crystal salt
- Tea bags
- Sweetener such as agave nectar or coconut sugar
- Flavored organic extra-virgin oil or favorite dressing in a small jar

# How to Introduce Raw Food to Friends and Family

You may find that your friends and family are a little reluctant to try raw foods. By considering these do's and don'ts, you can reduce their anxiety about how your new lifestyle may impact them:

- **Don't be preachy or pushy!** An aggressive attitude doesn't win friends or influence people. Instead, offer your family and guests delicious raw foods that you know they'll love and let them open the door and ask questions if they're interested in knowing the why and what of raw food.
- **Prepare recipes that include familiar and favorite foods.** Rather than forcing your food choices on others, make foods for others that you know they like. (Who doesn't love fresh salsa and guacamole or fresh veggies and dip?) If the raw options are delicious and you can avoid judging others on what they're eating, you may find that your family and friends are willing to try the new foods you prepare.
- **Introduce delicious green smoothies and juices**. Nutrient-packed smoothies and juices are delicious raw options for newbies. It's tough to argue the convenience of getting vital vitamins and minerals from these quick and easy treats — no matter how much raw a person chooses to consume each day. Even kids often enjoy making and consuming raw smoothies and juices.
- **Make an irresistible raw dessert or treat every week**. Choose a raw version of a traditional sweet treat that your family enjoys and invite the kids to help make it. Raw desserts are remarkably delicious because they're prepared with fresh whole ingredients.
- **Get your family involved in the kitchen**. Encourage others to help you prepare raw meals. People of almost all ages and cooking abilities can peel vegetables, decorate the table, and help choose menu items, and your family is more likely to enjoy eating a raw meal if they've helped make it.

- The raw food diet is based on the belief that uncooked and unprocessed food can help you to achieve better health and prevent diseases like heart disease and cancer. Some proponents claim that cooking breaks down the enzymes in uncooked or "live food" which aid in the digestion and absorption of nutrients.

## Some tips on incorporating raw foods into your diet:

- Start off slowly if you're going raw and swap out one regular meal a day for a raw food meal.
- Gradually work in more raw meals, depending on whether you go strictly raw or just want a few raw meals in your weekly diet.

# MAIN DISHES

# "Raw" Potato Pancakes with Apple Sauce

**Prep time: 20 mins || Total time: 20 mins**

**Vegan**

**Type: Main dish, appetizer**

**Serves: 2 as a light meal, 4 as an appetizer**

## Ingredients

- 1/3 cup pine nuts (ground fine)
- 1 clove garlic
- 1 large potato (I used a red potato)
- Water
- 1 tablespoon celtic sea or himalayan salt
- 1/2 purple onion (or other mild onion)
- 2 tablespoons dried rosemary
- 1 tablespoon olive oil

## Instructions

1. Put pine nuts in food processor and pulse until fine.
2. Set aside. With food processor running, drop in clove of garlic.
3. Switch blades and grate potato.
4. Put potato and garlic in a bowl filled with water and 1 tablespoon salt, let soak for 10 minutes, drain.

5. Meanwhile, chop the onion. Combine drained potato and garlic mixture, onion, pine nuts, rosemary and olive oil.

6. Place on dehydrator screens in pancake shapes, about 4″ across. Dehydrate at 145 for 45 minutes, then reduce heat and finish dehydrating at 116 for 2 more hours.

7. You want them to be fully dry. Remove with spatula and serve with raw apple sauce.

# Spinach Cashew Spread Three Ways

**Prep time: 20 mins || Total time: 20 mins**

**Type: Main dish**

**Serves: 2 as a light meal, 4 as an appetizer**

## Ingredients

BASE: SPINACH CASHEW "CHEESE" SPREAD

- 1 cup cashews, soaked at least 6 hours
- Juice from 1 1/2 Lemons
- 1/4 cup olive oil
- 1 shallot, chopped
- 1 clove garlic, chopped
- 1/2 cup sun dried tomatoes, chopped
- 1 pinch sea salt
- 2 handfuls of spinach, separated (aprox 2 cups firmly packed)

## Instructions

1. Drain cashews and place in food processor.
2. Add lemon juice and olive oil. Process until smooth.
3. Add shallot, and garlic. Process until well blended.
4. Add one handful of the spinach.

5. Continue to process until spinach is well incorporated.
6. Remove the mixture from the food processor.
7. Hand chop the remaining handful of spinach and stir in along with the sun dried tomatoes. This is the base spread.

OPTION 2: SPINACH VEGGIE QUICHE

Pumpkin Seed Pine Nut Crust

- 1 Carrot, finely chopped
- 1/2 Shallot
- 1 cup Pine Nuts
- 1/2 cup Pumpkin Seeds

## Instructions

1. Chop carrot into 1" pieces and place in food processor.
2. Process until very fine. Add 1/2 shallot, 1 cup Pine Nuts. Pulse a few times to start to blend. Add 1/2 cup Pumpkin Seeds.
3. Process until you have a formable mass but not so much that you lose the integrity of all the seeds. I like to see chunks of them. It also makes for a better texture!
4. Press into small pie plate. Dehydrate @ 145 for 1/2 hour.
5. Reduce heat and dehydrate 6 hours @ 114.

The higher temp will not compromise your food. The actual food temp never gets that high. This is a great technique I read about from Cafe Gratitude. It helps sweat the food, removes moisture and also decreases the dehydration time.

SPINACH VEGGIE QUICHE FILLING

## Ingredients

- 3/4 cup Spinach Cashew "Cheese" Spread
- 1 cup Cherry Tomatoes, halved
- 1 cup Pea Pods, Chopped into 1/2 " pieces
- 1/2 cup Sundried Tomatoes (softened and chopped)

## Instructions

1. Mix together all ingredients and place in prepared quiche crust. Refrigerate at least a couple of hours to set up.

SPINACH CASHEW ZUCCHINI PASTA

- Zucchini pasta (made from zucchini with spiral cutting blade)
- 1 cup cherry tomatoes, halved
- 1 cup pea pods, chopped

- 3/4 cup marinated, mushrooms
- 5 scallions, sliced
- 1/2 cup dried sun dried tomatoes, chopped
- 1/2 cup spinach cheese spread
- 1/4 cup watersea salt and pepper to taste

**Instructions**

1. To marinate mushrooms:
   - Cut the mushroom into slices about 1/4 to 1/2 inch thick.
   - Toss with 2 tablespoon of Nama Shoyu and 2 tablespoon oil and let sit for at least 1/2 hour.
2. Mix 1/2 cup Spinach Cheese Spread with 1/4 cup water to create sauce.
3. Add all other ingredients and toss.

# Raw Vegan Pineapple Salsa

**Prep time: 20 mins || Total time: 20 mins**

**Vegan**

**Type: Main dish, appetizer**

This tangy raw pineapple salsa has lots of vitamin C and other sweet and spicy flavors that make a delicious and healthy combination when served on the side of a main dish or as an appetizer with cucumber slices and/or dehydrated flax seed crackers.

**Ingredients:**

- ½ ripe pineapple, cut lengthwise.
- ¼ medium sized red onion, chopped finely.
- 2 medium sized jalapeno pepper, chopped finely.
- 1 medium sized green bell pepper, chopped finely.
- 1 Roma tomato, chopped finely.
- ¼ cup fresh cilantro leaves.

**Instructions:**

1. Cut off the top of the pineapple.
2. Carefully run a knife in a circle around the inside of the pineapple half an inch away from the skin while being careful not to penetrate the skin.
3. Once you've cut all the way around, cut the inside part across twice, thereby making four pieces.
4. Use a big and sturdy spoon to carefully scoop out the inside pieces, leaving the exterior of the pineapple an intact half-shell.
5. Cut off the tough fibrous core portion of the pineapple's interior pieces, and chop the softer part into small chunks.
6. Mix the chopped pineapple in with the other ingredients in a mixing bowl and squeeze gently to mix the flavors. Marinate the mixture for 10 minutes in its own juices.
7. Place the salsa in the hollowed out pineapple shell and serve.

# Savory Zucchini Wraps with Squash, Craisins and Sage "Cream"

**Prep time: 20 mins || Total time: 20 mins**

**Vegan**

**Type: Main dish, appetizer**

**Makes: 4-5 Wraps**

## SQUASH

### Ingredients

- 2 medium carnival or acorn squash
- 2 tablespoons olive oil salt and pepper

### Instructions

1. Advanced Preparation: The night before: peel and cube squash and place in cold, salted water.
2. Place in refrigerator overnight.
3. In the morning, drain, toss with 2 tablespoons olive oil, salt and pepper.
4. Place on screens in dehydrator. Dehydrate for 8 hours.

## WRAPS

## Ingredients

- 4 cups pureed zucchini
- 1 cup ground flax
- 2 tablespoons olive oil
- 2 tablespoons fine herbs

## Instructions

1. Combine all ingredients.
2. Spread on teflex sheets.
3. You want this to be at least 1/4" thick as zucchini will greatly reduce when dehydrated.
4. Place in dehydrator with squash.
5. You will want to peel the sheet off half way through the dehydration and move to screen.
6. Always place face up after you remove the sheet. You want these dried but not crisp.
7. Dehydration time will be around 8 hours at 116. Cut into quarters.

## SAGE "CREAM" SAUCE

## Ingredients

- 1 cup soaked cashews
- 1/2 cup pine nuts
- 2 tablespoons olive oil
- 1/2 lemon, juice from
- 2 tablespoons sage (I used dried)
- Salt and pepper to taste

## Instructions

1. In the morning, Put 1 cup cashews in water, place in refrigerator.
2. You will make the cream sauce just before assembling.
3. Place all ingredients in food processor and process until well blended and smooth.
4. You can also put this in the vitamix for an even smoother consistency.

## ASSEMBLY

- 1/2 cup craisins
- sage cream sauce
- zucchini wraps
- squash

## Instructions

1.  Spread sage cream sauce on wrap. Top with squash and craisins. Roll, cut and enjoy!

# Raw Vegan Sushi

**Prep time: 20 mins || Total time: 20 mins**

**Vegan**

**Type: Main dish,**

**Ingredients**

- 2 cup Sprouted Kamut
- 1 tablespoon Nama Shoyu
- 1 tablespoon Toasted Sesame Oil
- Sunflower Sprouts
- 2 Carrots
- 1/2 Cucumber
- 1 Portobello Mushroom, marinated in Nama Shoyu and olive oil
- Avocado, Sliced
- 2 Seaweed Sheets

**Instructions**

Step 1: Marinate the Mushrooms

1. Cut the portabello mushroom into slices about 1/4 to 1/2 inch thick.
2. Toss with 2 tablespoons of Nama Shoyu and 2 tablespoons oil and let sit for at least 1/2 hour.

Step 2: Make the Sushi

1. Process the kamut, Nama Shoyu and toasted sesame oil in a food processor until the kamut starts to break apart. Set aside.
2. Slice carrots and cucumber into match stick pieces, slice the avocado into 1/4 inch pieces. Set aside.
3. Lay your sheet of seaweed on the sushi matt.
4. Spread half the sheet with the kamut mixture.
5. Place the avocado, carrots, cucumber, sunflower sprouts (not pictured) and mushrooms on top of the kamut.

# Shredded Brussels and Fall Veg Salad with Garlicky Orange Tahini

**Prep time: 20 mins || Total time: 20 mins**

**Vegan**

**Type: Main dish**

**Serves: 4-6**

NOTES: You could easily mix up the veg here. I went with beets and sweet potatoes (because yay! Just found they're kind of awesome in their raw state), but kohl rabi, celery root, little turnips and fennel would all be so tasty.

**Salad Ingredients:**

- 1/2 lb brussels sprouts, trimmed + finely shredded/sliced
- 2 stalks celery, thinly sliced
- 2 small-medium beets, peeled + cut into thin matchsticks
- 1 small-medium sweet potato, peeled + cut into thin matchsticks
- 1 apple, cored + thinly sliced
- 1/2 small red onion, sliced into little slivers
- salt + pepper

dressing ingredients:

- 1 clove of garlic, peeled
- 1 tsp ground cumin
- 1 tsp grainy mustard (or dijon, whatevs)
- 1/3 cup raw tahini (or regular, NBD)
- juice of 1 orange (a generous 1/4 cup)
- raw honey/maple syrup/agave nectar to taste
- 1-2 tbsp extra virgin olive oil
- salt + pepper
- splashes of apple cider vinegar/water for thinning out (if necessary)

To finish:

- big handful flat leaf parsley, roughly chopped
- 1/3 cup raw pumpkin seeds

**Instructions**

1. In a large bowl, combine the sliced brussels sprouts, celery, beets, sweet potato shreds, sliced apple and red onion slivers.

2. Season all of that with some salt and pepper and toss. Set aside.
3. Make the dressing: combine all of the dressing ingredients in a blender on high until you have a smooth dressing that will coat the back of a spoon, in a decidedly thin way (you might have to add splashes of cider vinegar/water etc to get there). Check it for seasoning, adjust and set the dressing aside.
4. Pour the dressing onto the salad and toss it up. Garnish with the pumpkin seeds and parsley. I think it could hold up in its dressed state, sans apples, for a couple hours if you had to bring it somewhere. Just add the apples and garnish it up right before serving.

# Mango & Zucchini Lettuce Wraps

**Prep time: 20 mins || Total time: 20 mins**

**Type: Main dish, appetizer**

**Serves: 2 as a light meal, 4 as an appetizer**

These fresh lettuce wraps are a great party appetizer or light summer dinner!
Change up the veggies and herbs to your liking, and serve with generous drizzles
of dipping sauce.

## Ingredients

Romaine lettuce leaves

- ½ cup kelp noodles (optional)
- 1 zucchini, julienned
- ½ mango, thinly sliced
- 2-3 radishes, sliced into thin sticks
- ¼ cup chopped scallions
- 1-2 Thai red peppers, sliced
- Handful of fresh mint
- Edamame, baked tofu, or a protein of your choice
- Lime wedges, for serving
- Sriracha, for serving

Ginger soy dipping sauce:

- ¼ cup soy sauce
- 3 tablespoons rice vinegar
- 1 teaspoon minced fresh ginger
- 2 teaspoons honey or agave syrup
- ¼ teaspoon sesame oil
- Diced Thai chili pepper (optional)

## Instructions

1. Prep all your veggies and arrange on a platter. Mix the dipping sauce together.
2. Serve with lime wedges and sriracha, assembling your lettuce wraps to your liking.

# Raw Food "Burrito"

**Total: 20 mins || Prep: 20 mins**

**Yield: 6 to 8 servings**

**Vegan**

These raw food diet lettuce wraps have a hint of Mexican spiciness to them, hence the "burrito" simile. These wraps make a great entree for a raw food meal or a raw food potluck, and, because they're so easy and tasty, they're a great raw transitional food too. They're naturally gluten-free, of course.

## Ingredients

- 2 very ripe avocados
- 3 tomatoes (diced)
- 1/2 jalapeno pepper (diced)
- 2 tbsp. yellow onion (diced)
- 3 cloves fresh garlic (minced)
- 1/4 cup fresh cilantro (chopped)
- 3/4 cup corn (kernels from one ear raw corn)
- 2 tsp. fresh lime juice
- 6 to 8 large lettuce leaves

## Instructions

1. Gather the ingredients.
2. In a medium sized bowl, mash the avocado.
3. Add remaining ingredients and stir until well mixed.
4. Spread 2 to 3 tablespoons of this mixture onto lettuce leaves and wrap.
5. Serve and enjoy!

# Raw Carrot Falafel, Hemp-Seed Tabouli with Yellow Tomatoes and Mint

**Yield: 4 Servings**

**Vegan**

## Ingredients

Raw Carrot Falafel:

- 1 cup sesame seeds
- 1/2 teaspoon sea salt
- 1 1/2 cups carrot pulp from juicing or 1 1/2 cups finely grated carrot, squeezed firmly between paper towels to remove excess moisture
- 2 cloves garlic, minced
- 1 tablespoon freshly squeezed lemon juice
- 1/4 teaspoon ground cumin (optional)
- 2 tablespoons flax meal
- 1/4 cup fresh curly parsley

Hemp-Seed Tabouli with Yellow Tomatoes and Mint:

- 1 cup fresh parsley
- 1/2 cup fresh mint
- 1/4 teaspoon sea salt
- 4 medium yellow vine or Jersey tomatoes, chopped
- 1 cup shelled hemp seeds
- 2 tablespoons hemp oil
- 2 tablespoons freshly squeezed lemon juice

## Instructions

For the Falafel:

1. Grind the sesame seeds and sea salt in a food processor until finely ground.
2. Add the carrot pulp, garlic, lemon, cumin, if using, and flax, along with 1/3 cup of water. Process until the mixture is smooth.
3. Add the parsley to the processor and pulse to combine.
4. Shape the mixture into twelve small patties. Dehydrate at 115 F for 6 hours, flipping once through.
5. Alternatively, preheat the oven to 350. Bake the falafel for 15 minutes. Flip and cook for another 10 minutes, or until golden brown on both sides. Top with tangy tahini sauce (pg. 188), and serve.
6. Stored in an airtight container in the fridge, both dehydrated and baked falafel will keep for up to 4 days. They can also be frozen.

For the Tabouli:

1. In a food processor fitted with the "S" blade, process the parsley, mint, and sea salt until minced.
2. Transfer the herbs and salt to a large mixing bowl. Add the tomatoes, hemp seeds, hemp oil, and lemon juice. Mix well, and serve.
3. Stored in an airtight container in the fridge, the tabouli will keep for 2 days.

# Raw Vegan Power Zucchini Pasta with Hemp Seed Alfredo

**Prep Time: 20 minutes || Total Time: 20 minutes**

**Servings: 2 to 3**

Heaps of spiralized zucchini noodles and lemon-marinated veggies are tossed in a protein-packed vegan hemp seed alfredo and finished with a touch of vegan parmesan.

This dish is as fun to eat and satisfying as it is nourishing. It's packed with omega-3s, plant-based protein, and healthy fats.

## Ingredients

- 4 medium zucchini, ends trimmed
- 1 red bell pepper, seeded and julienned
- 2 heaping cups baby spinach, chiffonaded (very thinly sliced)
- 1 lemon, juiced (about 2 tablespoons)
- 1 recipe Hemp Seed Alfredo Sauce
- Small handful fresh basil leaves, chiffonaded (very thinly sliced)
- Sea salt, to taste
- Freshly ground black pepper, to taste

## Instructions

1. Use a spiralizer to spriralize the zucchini into pasta/noodles. Alternatively, use a vegetable peeler to shave the zucchini lengthwise, forming long, ribbon-like noodles.
2. Add the zucchini noodles, red bell pepper, and spinach to a large mixing bowl. Pour the lemon juice over the noodles and veggies and toss to coat. Let the noodles marinate for 10 minutes.
3. Meanwhile, prepare the Hemp Seed Alfredo Sauce.
4. Add the basil and pour as much of the Alfredo sauce as desired over the zucchini pasta. Toss to coat. Taste and season with sea salt and black pepper, to taste. If desired, sprinkle on a bit of vegan parmesan cheese*.
5. Divide between bowls and serve immediately.

Notes

*You can use store-bought vegan parmesan cheese or homemade. If you opt for homemade, simply add 1/4 cup raw cashews/almonds/hemp seeds, 2 to 4 tablespoons nutritional yeast flakes, and 1/4 to 1/2 teaspoon sea salt to a food processor and process for 10 to 15 seconds or until the texture resembles grated parmesan. Sprinkle on as much as desired and refrigerate leftovers.

**This recipe can easily be cut in half if you're looking to serve 1 to 2 people. Just remember to also cut the Hemp Seed Alfredo Sauce in half.

# Raw Vegan Bagels with Dill & Caper Cashew Cream Cheese

**Servings: 10 bagels**

**Nutrition (For one serving)**

**Ingredients**

Raw Vegan Bagels

- 1 cup quinoa flour
- 1 cup oat flour
- 1 cup ground almonds
- 2 tbsp psyllium powder
- 1 tbsp onion powder
- 1 tsp garlic powder
- 8 ozs zucchini (courgette) (peeled)
- ¼ cup cashews (soaked 20 mins to 1 hour)
- 2 tablespoons olive oil
- 1 tbsp maple syrup
- ¼ cup nutritional yeast
- 1 tbsp apple cider vinegar
- 1 cup water

Cashew Cream Cheese

- 1 cup cashews (soaked 20 mins to 1 hour)
- ½ cup water
- 1 teaspoon probiotic powder
- 1 tsp salt
- 1 tsp garlic powder
- 2 tsp onion powder
- ¼ cup capers minced
- 2 tbsp fresh dill minced

Assembly

- 1 cup Arugula
- 1/2 cup Baby tomatoes
- 1 Avocado
- 2 tbsp Irish moss gel (optional)

**Instructions**

Raw Vegan Bagels

1. Mix quinoa flour, oat flour, ground almond, psyllium powder, onion powder, garlic powder together in a large bowl.
2. In a high speed blender, process the zucchini, cashews, olive oil, maple syrup, nutritional yeast, apple cider vinegar and water until smooth and creamy.
3. Add the wet ingredients to the dry and mix well to combine. The mixture will thicken up after about 5 minutes. Once thickened, form into a ball and then roll into bagels, with the use of a mould if you have one. I prefer to make half bagels, so they don't need cutting at a later stage, but you can play around with this.
4. Dehydrate on a nonstick dehydrator tray for 6 to 8 hours at 115 degrees F. Take them off the nonstick sheet and dehydrate for a further 30 minutes to dry the bottoms.
5. Will store in a sealed container for up to 2 weeks.

Cashew Cream Cheese

1. Blend the cashews, water and probiotics in a high speed blender until smooth.
2. Transfer to a bowl, cover and leave in a warm place for 8 to 12 hours to ferment.
3. Once fermented, you'll see the mixture has small air bubbles and tastes slightly sour.
4. Mix in the salt, capers and dill and store in the fridge until ready to serve.
5. Will last up to a week in the fridge.

Assembly

1. Spread some caper dill cream cheese on each bagel half, then add avocado, tomatoes and rocket leaves.
2. I like to also grind some black or white pepper on top. These can be served open faced or as a sandwich.

**Calories: 327kcal, Carbohydrates: 29g, Protein: 10g, Fat: 20g, Saturated Fat: 2g, Sodium: 368mg, Potassium: 368mg, Fiber: 6g, Sugar: 3g, Vitamin A: 170IU, Vitamin C: 8.4mg, Calcium: 56mg, Iron: 2.9mg**

# Apple Carrot Cabbage Slaw

This colorful slaw is the perfect addition to your next potluck!

**Prep Time: 30 minutes || Total Time: 30 minutes**

**Servings: 2 quarts (8 cups)**

**Vegan**

**Ingredients**

- 2 apples
- 2 carrots
- 1 small head purple cabbage or 1/2 large head
- 1/2 cup tahini
- 2 tablespoons plain yogurt
- 1 tablespoon lemon juice
- 2 teaspoons spicy brown mustard
- 1 teaspoon maple syrup
- 1 teaspoon apple cider vinegar
- Salt and pepper to taste

**Instructions**

1. Rinse carrots, apples, and cabbage well. Cut into small strips and mix in a medium-sized bowl.
2. Make the dressing by mixing tahini, yogurt, lemon juice, mustard, maple syrup, apple cider vinegar, salt, and pepper together.
3. Mix the dressing into the bowl with the carrot, apple, cabbage mix.

# Rainbow Noodles with spicy jungle Peanut sauce

**Serving: 2**

**Ingredients**

Noodles:

- 1 sweet red pepper
- 2 zucchinis
- 1 carrot

Peanut sauce:

- 1 tablespoon raw jungle peanut butter
- 1 tablespoon miso
- Juice from ½ lemon
- 2 dates
- Chili powder, to taste
- 1 garlic clove
- 1 tablespoon nutritional yeast (optional)
- 1 teaspoon black sesame seeds (optional)
- Water or orange juice, as needed

Garnish:

- ¼ cilantro leaves
- 6 raw olives cut in half
- 1 tablespoon hemp seeds

**Instructions**

1.  To make the noodles: Cut the veggies lengthwise into thin strips on a mandolin or spiral slicer, then mix in a bowl and set aside.

2.  To make the sauce: blend all the ingredients until smooth, adding water or orange juice as needed to make it creamy.

3.  Assembly: pour the sauce onto the noodles and evenly coat. Give it a few minutes for the flavours to develop, and then sprinkle with hemp seeds, raw olives and cilantro leaves. Gobble it up!

# Butternut Tortilla, A Raw Vegan Omelette

**Serving: 2**

This butternut tortilla recipe is from Evie's Kitchen. Evie was so surprised when she tried this.

**Instructions**

- 200g butternut squash
- 30g flax seeds
- 4 cherry tomatoes
- 10g parsley
- 4 olives, pitted
- Pinch of Himalayan pink salt

**Instructions**

1. Finely grind the flax seeds. Quarter the tomatoes. Finely chop the parsley. Blend the squash with the flax to form a smooth paste.
2. In a bowl, mix the paste with the tomatoes, olives and parsley. Put a little parsley to one side to garnish.
3. Flatten the mixture into a thick pancake on a lined dehydrator tray. Sprinkle with the remaining parsley.
4. Dehydrate at 115°F/46°C for about five hours or until you can wait no more.

# Pear and Poppy Seeds Almond roulade
**Prep Time: 10 min || Total Time: 10 min**

**Cuisine: Vegan**

**Makes 3-4 servings**

**Ingredients**

Roulade 'dough':

- 1/2 cup (100gr) raw almonds

- 1/2 cup (100 gr) raw cashews fresh juice of 1 pear* (See notes)

- 1 TBSP coconut oil (melted)2-3 drops vanilla extract

- 1 TBSP raw honey (or maple syrup for vegetarian/vegan version)

* **To get the juice,** cut a ripe pear in 4 pieces and grated each, discarding the peel. Then put it in a colander on top of a bowl to separate the juice from the pulp. Use the juice to make the dough and the pulp for the filling.

**Instructions**

1. First processed the almonds in a blender to grind them finely.

2. Take them out and do the same thing with the cashews. Then mixed them together with the rest of the ingredients until completely incorporated.

3. Spread the 'dough' on a sushi mat covered with cling film (it helps to roll it well).

For the filling:

- 100gr poppy seeds fresh pulp of 1 pear

- zest of 1 lemon

- 1 TBSP honey (or maple syrup for vegetarian/vegan version)

**Instructions**

1. Mix together all the ingredients by hand.

2. Use a very sweet and very ripe pear, but if your pear is not sweet enough you might want to add a bit more honey in the filling. Fear not to taste the filling at this stage and to adjust it to your liking.

3. Spread the pear-poppy seed mix on top of the layer of 'dough' and gently began to roll it, applying slight pressure.

4. Once finished, place it in the freezer for about 10-15 minutes then moved it to the fridge until ready to serve. It should be ready to be gone in about an hour or so.

# Rawsagne

**Prep Time: 4 hrs || Total Time: 4 hrs**

**Cuisine: Vegan**

**Makes 3-4 servings**

This is not a fast recipe! It needs a bit of preparation. Start the cheese at least a day before. Soak the sundried tomatoes and goji berries 2 hours before you start making the recipe. The courgette needs soaking for 30 minutes but you can make the sauce during this time. If you want to dehydrate the dish, add another 2-3 hours to the recipe.

'Ricotta' style cheese:

I use fermented cheese in my Rawsagne, but if this feels still a bit advanced to you, then just leave out the fermenting stage. It will still be very nice.

## Ingredients

- 2 cups Macademia nuts (soaked for 30 mins)
- 1 cup water
- 1 tsp probiotics (buy any good quality lactose free probiotics. If they come in a capsule, just remove the capsule)

## Instructions

1. Blend all ingredients in a high speed blender.

2.  You want the mixture to be as smooth as possible, but keep in mind that macademia nuts are very fibrous, so a bit of grain is normal and wanted.
3.  Fill the mix into a cheesecloth or nut milk bag and place it into a sieve on top of a bowl. Place a heavy object on top. I use a large killner jar filled with water.
4.  This will squeeze out any excess liquid while the mix is fermenting.
5.  Cover the whole thing with a clean tea towel and leave to ferment in a warm place (next to your dehydrator is ideal) for 24-36 hours.
6.  Now stir in the rest of the ingredients below.

- 1/4 tsp sea salt
- 2-3 tsp nutritional yeast

If you've decided not to ferment your cheese, then add 1 tbsp lemon juice, ¼ tsp sea salt and 1 tbsp nutritional yeast to the first three ingredients and blend all together until smooth instead of the fermenting and stage two ingredients.

Spread the mix into a shallow bowl or onto a large plate, cover and keep in the fridge for a few hours to let the mix set.

**Ingredients for the layers:**

- 2 medium courgette (Slice the courgette length wise on a mandoline into thin layers. Place in a bowl with salted water. After 30 mins remove the courgette and pat dry with kitchen with kitchen paper)
- 3 cups/100g of baby (spinach Wash and dry the spinach, then add 2 tbsp of olive oil and massage the oil into the spinach until it wilts.)
- 200g of organic mushrooms, cleaned and sliced thinly
- 2 tbsp of unpasteurized kalamata olives, sliced thinly

For the sauce:

- 3 medium tomatoes
- 3/4 cup/55g sundried tomatoes (soaked for 2 hours, rinsed and drained)
- 1/4 cup/20g goji berries (soaked for 2 hours, drained – reserve the liquid and use in a smoothy!)
- 1 tsp onion powder
- 1 garlic clove
- 2 tbsp chopped fresh or frozen basil
- 1 tsp dried mixed herbs
- 1 tbsp olive oil
- salt and freshly ground black pepper to taste

**Instructions**

- Blend all ingredients until you get a fairly smooth, thick sauce.

**Instructions for the layering:**

1. I use a round glass baking dish approximately 22cm/8.5" diameter. But you could also use a square dish. Start with covering the base with courgette slices.
2. Add one third of the tomato sauce and spread out to cover the courgette. Add slices of mushrooms and olives.
3. Now spoon on half of the macademia cheese. I use a teaspoon for this and basically place dollops of cheese next to each other with a little space in between.
4. Now add half of the spinach to cover the cheese and press down with your hands. Repeat these steps one more time, starting with the courgette.
5. m Eat straight away or dehydrate for 2-3 hours until nicely warmed through.
6. You can also warm this in the oven. Set the temperature to the lowest setting and leave the oven door open slightly so it doesn't get too hot inside.
7. If you like you can sprinkle it with some Almond Parmesan

# Tahini Sauce

Portobello Mushroom stuffed with Avocado & Heirloom Tomato slices then topped with a tahini sauce and a sprig of fresh thyme

**Ingredients**

Tahini Sauce:

- 1/2 cup filtered water
- 1/2 cup cold pressed extra virgin olive oil (or 1/2 cup more water)
- 1/3 cup tahini
- 1/2 red bell pepper or 1 tomato
- 1/4 small onion
- The juice of 1 lemon
- 3 mejool dates
- 2 tablespoons raw spicy mustard
- 2 teaspoons kelp powder
- 1 teaspoon garlic powder or 1-2 cloves garlic
- 1 teaspoon sea salt
- a dash of cayenne

**Instructions**

1. Mix in a blender until creamy

# Vegan Sprouted Lentil Chili.

**Prep Time: 10 min || Total Time: 10 min**

**Cuisine: Vegan**

**Makes 3-4 servings**

**Ingredients**

- 3 roma tomatoes diced small
- 3 celery stalks finely diced
- 1/2 large red bell pepper diced small
- 1/2 red onion diced small
- 1 cup sprouted red lentils
- 1/2 cup sprouted green lentils

**Instruction**

1. Place the following in a large bowl

**Sauce ingredients**

- 1 cup soak water from the sundried tomatoes & date
- 1 cup of sundried tomatoes (soaked)
- 1/2 large red bell pepper
- 1 date (soaked)
- 1 stalk celery
- 2 tablespoons onion powder
- 2 tablespoons raw apple cider vinegar
- 1 tablespoon nama shoyu (optional, not raw)
- 1 teaspoon garlic powder
- 1 teaspoon oregano
- 1 teaspoon chili powder
- 1/2 teaspoon cayenne pepper
- sea salt to taste

**Instructions**

2. Blend above ingredients until creamy & pour over vegetable mixture & let marinate for several hours so the flavors will blend.
3. Garnish with raw vegan sour cream & scallions & serve with raw crackers or chips.

Note: To make the sour cream I blended truly raw soaked cashews, lemon juice, raw apple cider vinegar, a little filtered water & sea salt.

# Nana Brownies

**Prep Time: 10 min || Total Time: 10 min**

**Cuisine: Vegan**

**Makes 3-4 servings**

## Ingredients

- 1 1/3 cup almonds
- 1 cup walnuts
- 2 tablespoons banana powder (dried banana used food processor to make powder)
- 1/4 teaspoon vanilla bean powder (dried a vanilla bean put in food processor to make powder)
- 2 pinches himalayan salt
- Pinch of cinnamon, optional
- 1/4 cup pitted, packed dates
- 1 1/2 teaspoons water

## Instructions

1. Grind the almonds into flour in a food processor.
2. Add all remaining ingredients and grind until the dates are broken down.
3. Make sure the mixture holds together when pressed in your hand, otherwise add a touch more water.
4. Press into the bottom of an 8x8" pan.

Frosting

## Ingredients

- 1 cup mashed banana
- 2 teaspoons maple syrup (not raw)
- 2 tablespoons banana powder
- 2 tablespoons lucuma powder (this is a sweetener I order Online) you could use sweetener of choice. Agava, Honey, Maple Syrup
- 1/2 teaspoon pure vanilla extract
- 1/2 teaspoon lemon juice
- Few pinches turmeric for colour
- 8 tablespoons melted coconut oil

## Instructions

1. Blend all but the coconut oil in a blender until smooth.
2. Add the oil and blend to incorporate.
3. Spread the frosting over the bars. Sprinkle chopped pecans on top (optional).
4. Chill for at least 4 hours, or until the frosting is set.
5. Slice into bars.

# Raw Mushroom Stroganoff

**Prep Time: 10 min || Total Time: 10 min**

**Cuisine: Vegan**

**Makes 3-4 servings**

**Ingredients**

- 12-16 ounces of sliced mushrooms
- 4 or 5 chopped scallions organic olive oil
- red wine vinegar
- 1 tablespoon of onion powder

**Instructions**

1. Marinate 12-16 ounces of sliced mushrooms along with some finely sliced onions or & 4 or 5 chopped scallions in a small amount of cold pressed organic olive oil, nama shoyu(optional), red wine vinegar & a tablespoon of onion powder (just enough to get them wet)
2. Let them marinate for a few hours.

**The sauce**

- 1/2 cup cashews soaked & rinsed
- 1/2 cup of the marinated mushrooms & onions
- 1/2 cup filtered water
- 1/4 cup of the marinade & juice from the mushrooms
- 1 celery stick (chopped)
- 1 tablespoon raw miso
- 1 tablespoon nama shoyu (optional)
- 1 tablespoon onion powder
- 1/2 teaspoon garlic powder
- 1/2 teaspoon paprika
- 1/4 teaspoon thyme
- 1/4 teaspoon fresh cracked pepper

**Instruction**

1. Blend until creamy then add in the marinated mushrooms

# BBQ Sauce

**Prep Time: 10 min || Total Time: 10 min**

**Cuisine: Vegan**

**Makes 3-4 servings**

## Ingredients

- 1 cup fresh tomatoes
- ¼ cup onion, chopped
- ½ sun-dried tomatoes, chopped
- ½ tsp minced garlic
- ¾ tsp minced jalapeno
- 4 fresh basil leaves
- ½ cup mendjool dates pitted
- olive oil or fresh tomato juice for blending
- ¼ cup Nama Shoyu or sea salt. (I used Tamari)
- 1 Tbsp. olive oil

## Instructions

1. Combine all together except last 3 in blender and blend until smooth.
2. Add a little olive oil or tomato juice if sauce is too thick.
3. Stir in last 2 ingredients. Keeps in fridge for 2 days.

# Raw Vegan Caramel Cacao Pecan Clusters

**Prep Time: 10 min || Total Time: 10 min**

**Makes 3-4 servings**

## Ingredients

Caramel

- 10 soft medjool dates
- 1/4 cup water
- 1/4 cup liquid sweetener of your choice
- 3 tablespoons coconut butter
- 1 1/2 teaspoons vanilla extract or a whole vanilla bean
- a pinch of sea salt

## Instructions

1. Blend until creamy. I also put mine through a strainer to make it extra creamy

Chocolate topping

- 1/4 cup of coconut oil (will melt in a warm room)
- 1/3 cup of raw cacao
- 4 tablespoons of liquid sweetener of choice (date paste, raw agave, etc)
- 1 pinch of sea salt

## Instruction

Lay out raw pecans in a little cluster on some parchment or wax paper. Top with caramel & chocolate topping. I store mine in the freezer so they keep longer.

# Falafel or Nori Sticks

**Prep Time: 10 min || Total Time: 10 min**

**Ingredients**

- 2 cups carrots (2 med/large carrots)
- 1/2 cup sunflower seeds - soak min 20 min, rinse, drain
- 1/4 cup buckwheat - soak min 20 min, rinse, drain
- 1/4 cup tahini
- 1/4 cup fresh parsley
- 1-2 cloves of garlic
- 2 Tbsp sun dried tomatoes (softened)
- 1 Tbsp lemon juice
- 1 Tbsp psyllium husks
- 2 Tbsp flax seeds
- 1 Tbsp dried onion bits
- 2 Tsp curry powder
- 1/2 Tsp cumin
- Sea Salt

**Instructions**

1. Process in your food processor until broken down and no large pieces. Mixture should stick together easily.
2. Form small patties - if mixture is a bit wet then coat the patties in a mix of sesame seeds and ground flax.
3. Cut nori sheets in half
4. Spread mixture evenly - roll up and moisten the end of the roll so it all sticks together.
5. Dehydrate at 115F until dry and crispy (for the nori sticks) and until crunchy on the outside soft on the inside for the patties.

# Apricot Energy Bites

## Ingredients

- 1 cup cashews
- 1 cup dried coconut
- 1/2 cup dried apricots
- 1/2 cup soft pitted dates
- 1 Tbsp lemon juice
- 1 Tbsp coconut oil
- 1 tsp vanilla extract
- pinch of salt

## Instructions

1. Use your food processor - put all the ingredients in and process until mixture is similar to a dough.
2. 1 Tsp per bite (or more if you want bigger ones)
3. Roll in coating of your choice (I used coconut this time

# Raw vegan ranch

## Ingredients

- 6oz raw cashews
- 2 key limes (peel and all)
- 2T rice vinegar
- 2 garlic cloves
- 1/2 t sea salt
- Italian seasoning to taste
- 1/4 cup of onion
- 1T hemp hearts
- 1 cup plant milk of choice or water
- 3/4 of a zucchini

## Instructions

1. Blend and enjoy (refrigerate what's left over for your next salad.)
2. (I poured it over half a head of shredded cabbage and 5 chopped Roma tomatoes)

# Coconut Tahini Bites

## Ingredients

- 2 cups raw coconut chips (the dried ones)
- 1/3 cup tahini
- 6 soft dates
- 2 Tbsp maple syrup
- 1-2 Tbsp coconut oil
- pinch of salt

--- this is a great base for any energy bite---

- zest from a large orange
- 1/4 cup cacao powder
- 1 tsp cinnamon
- 1/2 tsp mesquite powder
- 1/4 tsp nutmeg

## Instructions

1. Process in your food processor until mixture will stick together when pressed.
2. Roll into the size you want - roll in coating of your choice - I used hemp hearts.

# Raw cake Mango-Apple

## Ingredients

Base:

- 150g almonds
- 50g chia seeds
- 50g sunflower seeds
- 200g fresh dates
- 25g cocoa
- (25g of coconut oil - optional)
- 1-2 tablespoons of water or soak dates
- a little cinnamon

## Instructions

1. Knead and press with a spoon into the bottom of the cake pan.

Filling:

- 450g mango
- 450g apples
- 300g cashew nuts
- 150g of coconut oil (or more nuts for WFPB)
- 45g agave syrup (optional because fruits are sweet enough)
- juice of one small lemon
- a little cardamom

## Instructions

2. Blend only fruit, cardamom, lemon juice (*and agave), then add gradually cashews and coconut oil (*or more nuts).
3. Take away couple of tablespoons to garnish and refrigerate.
4. Pour the cream over the base and freeze, then garnish with mango, raw chocolate (cocoa, coconut oil, agave syrup-*or just raw cocoa for WFPB) and cream.
5. The cake pan is 26cm. For a higher height double filling mixture or at least 50% more.

# Raw Vegan Apple Pie

**Prep time: 20 minutes**

Crust:

- 1 cup raw almonds
- 1 cup raw walnuts
- 2 TBS ground flax seed
- 8 dates
- 3 tablespoons water
- A few dashes of sea salt

Sauce:

- 4-5 large apples
- 1 TBS ground flax seed
- 2 TBS chia seed
- 1 TBS raw almonds
- 7 dates
- ½ tsp cinnamon
- Dash of allspice and nutmeg
- ½ tsp raw apple cider vinegar
- A few dashes of sea salt
- 1 cup water

**Instructions**

1. Combine all ingredients for the crust in a food processor until crumbly.
2. Press mixture into pie pan and stick it in the fridge while you make the sauce.
3. De-core and blend two of the apples with the remaining ingredients—the mixture should be smooth, taste it to ensure the flavor—should be creamy, sweet and a bit salty.
4. Take the two remaining apples and thin slice and line bottom of the pie crust in the pan and sprinkle with salt and cinnamon (bottom layers don't need to be pretty) make 2-3 layers of apples like this pouring the sauce in between each layer.
5. Design the top layer to your liking and garnish with nuts or spices. Chill in fridge overnight.

# kimchi

**Prep Time: 10 min || Total Time: 10 min**

**Ingredients**

Cabbage

- Napa cabbage – ½ large head (or 1 small)
- 1 teaspoon salt

**Instructions**

1. Separate and wash cabbage leaves thoroughly. Tear or slice into small pieces.
2. Gently massage 1 teaspoon of salt onto cabbage leaves and let sit while you prepare the seasoning paste.
1. Water will start to release from the cabbage to become the brine.

Seasoning paste

- ¼ bell pepper or chili (for more spice), roughly chopped or julienned (approx. 1/3 cup)
- 1 tablespoon minced fresh garlic
- 1 tablespoon minced fresh ginger
- 1 tablespoon minced fresh green onions
- 1 ½ teaspoons red pepper flakes (more if you like spicy, less if you don't)
- 2 teaspoons agave
- 1 teaspoon salt

**Instructions**

Process all ingredients in a food processor, forming a paste. Wearing gloves, use your hands to rub

seasoning paste evenly over all cabbage leaves. Massage vigorously to release more water and create the kimchi brine.

ASSEMBLY

- ¼ cup julienned carrot
- ¼ cup red cabbage, finely shredded on mandoline

**Instructions**

1. Add carrot and red cabbage to napa cabbage mixture.

2. Transfer seasoned cabbage leaves into a glass container (mason jar, etc.) and use firm pressure with your (gloved) hands to push down on the cabbage leaves as they stack up inside the jar.
3. Pour any extra liquid that may have accumulated during the mixing process into the bottle as well - this will become the kimchi brine.
4. Some liquid will also come out of the cabbage leaves as you press them into the container. The cabbage should be completely covered by the brine.
5. Leave about 2 inches of room at the top of the jar before capping it tightly with a lid.
6. Allow kimchi to sit at room temperature (away from sunlight) for 2-3 days, burping the jar once a day to relieve pressure.
7. After 2-3 days, your kimchi is ready to eat, and can be moved to the fridge to store.

# kimchi dumplings

**Ingredients; Cilantro coconut wrapper**

- 1 ½ cups young coconut meat, chopped
- 2-3 tbs cilantro spinach juice
- Water as needed
- Pinch salt

**Instructions: Cilantro coconut wrapper**

1. Blend above ingredients until completely smooth.
2. Spread mixture in a thin, even layer over a non-stick sheet and dehydrate for 6-8 hours. Typically yields 1-1 ½ sheets.
3. If wrappers are brittle or too dry, gently brush with water and let sit for 15-20 minutes until the water has been absorbed.
4. Repeat until the wrappers can be folded or bent without cracking.
5. In humid climates, simply leaving the coconut wrappers out at room temperature (not brushing with water) is usually sufficient to soften the wrappers to an appropriate consistency.
6. Cut each sheet into even squares. 3 ½ inch squares yield a typical wonton or dumpling.
7. For storage, layer pieces of parchment in between the coconut wrappers, place in an airtight container and store in the refrigerator.
8. Let wrappers sit at room temperature for a few minutes before attempting to fold them.

**Ingredients: kimchi filling**

- ½ cup cashews, soaked 1-2 hours
- 1 ½ teaspoons tamari
- 1 ½ teaspoons sesame oil*
- 1 ½ teaspoons raw tahini
- ½ teaspoon agave
- ½ cup pre-made kimchi, drained

**Instructions; kimchi filling**

1. Process the kimchi, cashews, tamari, oil, tahini, and agave in a food processor until a chunky consistency is achieved.
2. Adjust seasoning to taste.

**Ingredients; Sesame ginger foam**

- ½ cup ginger juice
- ¼ cup sesame oil

- 1 1⁄2 teaspoons agave
- 1 teaspoon lecithin

## Instructions; Sesame ginger foam

1. Dissolve lecithin in ginger juice prior to blending.
2. Using an immersion blender, combine all ingredients until a thick foam appears on the surface. Froth the mixture again for each serving.
3. Only use the foam for plating.

## Ingredients; Purple cabbage puree

- 1⁄4 head of purple cabbage
- 1⁄2 cup kimchi brine
- water as needed to blend
- 1⁄4 teaspoon salt
- 1⁄4 cup grape seed oil
- 1⁄4 teaspoon xanthan gum

## Instructions; Purple cabbage puree

1. Slice cabbage thin. Toss with salt and let sit until soft. Purée salted cabbage, water, and kimchi brine until
2. completely smooth. Pass through a fine mesh strainer and return strained liquid to a clean blender. Add grape seed oil, xanthan gum, blend, and let rest 5-10 minutes before using.

## ASSEMBLY

1. Lay coconut wrappers out on a cool workspace. Dab very lightly with water.
2. Place a small amount of kimchi filling on each- about 1 tablespoon, and pull edges up around filling to form a dumpling, then press to seal.
3. Garnish plate with Purple Cabbage Purée and black sesame seeds. Garnish dumplings with Sesame Ginger Foam and micro greens.

# Orange Chia Pudding with Raspberries

**Prep Time: 10 min || Total Time: 10 min**

**Cuisine: Vegan**

**Makes 1-2 servings**

## Ingredients

- 2 cups cashews (soaked)
- 1 cup almond milk
- 1/2 cup liquid sweetener (like date paste or raw honey)
- 1/2 cup chia seeds
- The juice of 1 orange
- 1/4 cup coconut butter
- 1 teaspoon vanilla extract or 1 vanilla bean

## Instructions

1. Place all Ingredients except the chia seeds in a high speed blender & mix until creamy. Place mixture in a bowl & add the chia seeds.
2. Stir for several minutes. It will seem watery, but will thicken up a lot after you refrigerate for an hour. (You might even need to add a little more almond milk after it is chilled).
3. Serve with your favorite berries

# DESSERT

# Raw Key Lime Pie Bars

**Prep Time: 15 mins**

**Yield: 9 large or 12 small**

**Category: Dessert**

**Vegan**

**Ingredients**

BASE

- 1 cup raw macadamia nuts
- 3/4 cup unsweetened shredded coconut
- 3/4 cup dates
- pinch of salt

FILLING

- 1 1/2 cups raw macadamia nuts (or raw cashew nuts), soaked overnight in water (*see note)
- 1/2 cup fresh squeezed key lime juice (or regular lime juice)
- 1/2 cup light coconut milk (from a can)
- 1/4 cup coconut oil
- 1/4 cup brown rice syrup (or maple syrup)
- 1 tsp matcha powder or green food color (optional)

**Instructions**

1. Line an 8×8 inch pan with parchment paper.
2. In a food processor, pulse together the macadamia nuts, shredded coconut, dates, and salt until it forms a sticky dough.
3. Press into an even layer at the bottom of your pan. Place in the fridge while you prepare the filling.
4. Drain the soaked macadamia nuts. Add the nuts, lime juice, coconut milk, coconut oil, brown rice syrup, and matcha powder to your food processor, or high-speed blender.
5. Blend together until it forms a thick cream. (About 3-5 minutes in a food processor, or 2-3 minutes in a high-speed blender)
6. Pour your key lime mixture into your pan and spread evenly.
7. Place in the freezer to firm up for 2 hours, or overnight.
8. Cut into squares and serve

Serving Size: 1 small bar

Calories: 363, Sugar: 9g, Fat: 34g, Saturated Fat: 14g, Carbohydrates: 15g, Fiber: 5g, Protein: 4g

# Raw Vegan Lemon Cheesecake

**Category: Dessert**

**Yield: 10**

**Ingredients**

Crust:

- 1 cup pitted dates
- ½ cup nuts (any nuts will do)
- 2 tbsp coconut oil

Filling:

- 2 cups cashews
- ⅓ cup coconut butter
- grated zest of 2 lemons
- squeezed juice of one lemon
- 4 tbsp maple syrup
- ½ tsp turmeric

**Instructions**

1. Soak the cashews in cold water overnight. Or half an hour in boiling water (don't cook). Drain and rinse before starting to make the cake filling.
2. Prepare the crust before the filling. Measure dates, nuts and 2 tbsp of coconut oil in a blender and blend to a sticky paste.
3. Press the crust paste with your fingers in a 6-inch spring form and put them in the freezer to wait for the filling to be prepared.
4. Put all the rest of the ingredients in a cleaned blender and pulse until the mixture in silky and smooth.
5. Pour the filling over the crust and let to set in the fridge for overnight or if you are in a hurry, for a couple of hour in the freezer.

# Gluten-Free Vegan Vanilla Bean and Blueberry Chia Pudding

**Prep Time: 5 minutes || Inactive Time: 1 hour**

**Total Time: 1 hour 5 minutes**

**Vegan**

**Yields: 2**

**Calories: 199**

This healthy plant-based Vanilla Bean and Blueberry Chia Seed Pudding is an easy recipe to make with only 5 clean, real food ingredients and it can be prepared in less than 5 minutes. It's a perfect healthy breakfast or snack to meal prep, is kid-friendly and everyone will love it!

## Ingredients

- 1 cup homemade almond milk
- 1/2 cup organic blueberries
- 1/4 cup organic chia seeds
- 2 tablespoons organic maple syrup
- 1/2 teaspoon organic vanilla bean powder

## Instructions

1. Add all ingredients to a 16-ounce or larger mason jar and seal it very tightly.
2. Shake it vigorously until everything is mixed well and put it in the refrigerator for about an hour, or until it thickens to your preference.
3. Stir it up before serving and add additional blueberries on top, if you prefer.

## Notes

- Homemade Almond Milk. This is my milk of preference, however, you can use your favorite non-dairy milk in the same amount.
- Blueberries. I used fresh organic blueberries, but frozen organic blueberries will also work. The color might be a little darker with frozen blueberries but it will taste the same. For more nutrients and healing benefits, you can also use organic wild blueberries per Medical Medium recommendations.

- Maple Syrup. This can be reduced and even omitted if you prefer a less sweet chia pudding. For example, sometimes if my blueberries are really sweet I won't add the maple syrup at all.
- Vanilla Bean Powder. I like to use organic vanilla bean powder in my no-bake recipes because of the added alcohol in vanilla extract. However, you can substitute the vanilla bean powder with organic pure vanilla extract in the same amount. In addition, if you need this recipe to be 100% Medical Medium compliant, you can also substitute with alcohol-free vanilla extract.
- Serving Size: This recipe will make 16-ounces. Nutritional information is calculated at (1) serving being (1) cup.

**Serving: 1svg | Calories: 199kcal | Carbohydrates: 28g | Protein: 4g | Fat: 8g | Sodium: 168mg | Fiber: 9g | Sugar: 16g | Calcium: 306mg**

# Raw Peanut Butter Cookies

**Prep Time: 10 Mins || Total Time 10 Mins**

**Serves: 20 cookies**

**Vegan**

Soft, chewy raw peanut butter cookies are so fluffy and moist in the center after a few hours in the dehydrator. An easy snack to make for peanut butter lovers! Substitute any nut butter to make your favorite cookie.

## Ingredients

- ½ cup almond flour
- ¼ cup coconut flour (simply process desiccated coconut until extra fine)
- ¼ cup peanut butter (raw, unsalted, unsweetened)
- ¼ cup almond milk
- 2 tablespoons coconut nectar, agave or liquid sweetener of choice
- ½ teaspoon vanilla bean (optional)
- pinch sea salt (optional)

Superfood Boost (optional):

- Add 1 tablespoon Organic Burst Maca Powder

## Instructions

1. Sift the coconut flour into a mixing bowl, then add almond flour and remove any clumps.
2. Add all remaining ingredients and stir together until evenly combined.
3. Let the mixture sit for a few minutes until the dough thickens a bit.
4. Transfer mixing bowl to the refrigerator for 1-2 hours. This step to firm up the cookie dough helped me score the tops of the cookies a lot easier.
5. Scoop out about 1 tablespoon of cookie dough, roll into balls and flatten slightly.
6. Place cookies onto a parchment paper lined tray.
7. Score the tops of each cookie by using a fork to press down on the cookie balls, further flattening them about ½ inch thick. I found that dipping the fork into a bowl of water helped me score the tops easier.
8. Sprinkle sea salt over the tops of the cookies.
9. Transfer cookies to a teflex tray and place in the dehydrator for 12-16 hours. Dehydrate for longer if you want to store them for a longer shelf life.
10. Optional: To make nuttier butters, spread additional peanut butter between two cookies.

11. Store cookies in the refrigerator.

NOTES

Substitutions:

- For a lower fat alternative, replace almond flour with oat or buckwheat flour (grind rolled oats/buckwheat groats into flour with food processor).
- Replace peanut butter with almond, cashew, sunflower seed butter.
- Replace almond milk with any plant-based milk; soy, cashew or coconut milk.
- If you do not own a dehydrator, bake on lowest heat for several hours in the oven until outside is dry and the center is still soft.

# Raw Vegan Carob or Chocolate Donuts

**Vegan**

This raw vegan recipe features yummy raw carob or chocolate donuts! This naturally sweet and fully raw treat is healthy, nutritionally dense and rich in antioxidants.

**Ingredients:**

Donut:

- 1/4 cup raw almonds
- 1/4 cup raw pecans
- 1/2 cup dehydrated unsweetened coconut shreds
- 1/4 cup sprouted whole buckwheat
- 1/4 cup raw carob powder or raw chocolate powder (you may have to order this online)
- Dash of sea salt
- 1 cup soaked Medjool dates (use soaking water below)

Carob or Chocolate Almond Butter Glaze:

- 3 tbsp raw smooth almond butter
- 1 tbsp raw carob powder or raw chocolate powder (you may have to order this online)
- 2 tbsp date soaking water

Optional Toppings:

- Raw cacao nibs, chopped raw nuts or shredded coconut

**Instructions:**

1. For the donuts, blend or food process the almonds, pecans, coconut shreds, sprouted buckwheat, salt, and raw carob or cacao powder until finely ground.
2. Add in dates and pulse until dough forms.
3. Remove from blender and shape into donuts or roll in your palms to make donut holes.
4. Set aside to dry out or dehydrate at less than 117 degrees F for an hour or so to firm up the exterior of your donuts.
5. For the glaze, mix together the almond butter, raw carob or cacao powder, and date soaking water to form a smooth paste.
6. Spread glaze on top of doughnuts or dip them in it.
7. Top with sprinkles of raw nuts or shredded coconut.
8. Set the donuts in the fridge to firm up or eat them right away.

# Lemon Coconut Energy Bites

**Prep Time: 20 minutes | Total Time: 20 minutes**

**Vegan**

These zesty bites are filled with energizing nutrients for a quick boost.

**Ingredients**

- 10 Medjool dates pits removed
- 1/2 cup rolled oats gluten-free if needed
- 1/2 cup walnuts
- 1/2 cup unsweetened shredded coconut plus more for topping
- Juice from 1 lemon about 2 tablespoons
- Zest from 1 lemon about 1 teaspoon
- 2 tablespoons dairy-free milk
- 2 tablespoons flax seed meal
- 1 teaspoon vanilla extract
- 1 teaspoon turmeric
- 1/8 teaspoon black pepper
- Sunflower seeds optional for topping

**Instructions**

1. If your dates are dry, soak in warm water for a few minutes until slightly soft and sticky.
2. In a food processor or powerful blender mix together all ingredients until well-combined.
3. Scoop a rounded teaspoon and roll mixture into a bite-sized ball. Repeat until all the mixture is used — you should have roughly 25-30 balls.
4. Roll balls in extra shredded coconut, sunflower seeds, or enjoy as is. Store in an air-tight container in the refrigerator for up to 5 days or the freezer for up to 1 month.

# Raw vegan "Alfredo" with zucchini noodles

## Ingredients

Alfredo Sauce:

- 1 cup cashews
- 1 medium white onion
- 2-3 minced garlic cloves
- 1-2 lime
- 1 tsp of oregano, thyme, rosemary, and basil. Or 3-4 tsp of Italian seasoning
- 2 tsp of salt
- 1/4 c of water or nondairy milk
- 1 tbsp of nutritional yeast

## Instructions

1. Soak cashews. (I soaked mine for 8-9 hours while I was at work)
2. Put cashews, and the rest of the ingredients into the blender and blend until a creamy consistency.
3. Add more seasonings and salt to your liking, as well as feel free to add more nutritional yeast.
4. This is an estimate recipe because I didn't really measure anything but I was using a half tsp so this is an approximate of what I used.
5. I also peeled the zucchini skin so it looked more like real pasta but the skin has a lot of fiber and benefits so you to you if you want to leave it or take off.

# Raw Coconut Lime Pie

**Prep Time: 10 min || Total Time: 10 min**

**Category: Dessert**

**Cuisine: Vegan**

**Makes (4) 4" tarts or (1) 9" tart**

**Ingredients**

Coconut Crust

- 1 1/2 cup shredded coconut (unsweetened)
- 1/4 cup flax meal
- 6 large dates, pitted
- 1 tbsp coconut oil, melted
- 1 tsp vanilla
- pinch of salt

Coconut Lime Filling

- 1 cup fresh, young coconut meat (about two coconuts) *
- 1 small avocado
- 1/3 cup freshly squeezed lime juice
- 1/4 cup + 2 tbsp coconut nectar, or maple syrup
- 1 tsp coconut extract
- zest of 2 lime
- pinch of salt
- 2 tbsp coconut oil, melted

**Instructions**

1.) To make the crust, blend together the ingredients for the tart shell in a food processor until moist and sticks together when pressed.
2.) Divide into four 4" tart shells (or one 9" shell) and press evenly into shell, filling the bottoms and sides. Place in the refrigerator while preparing the filling.
3.) To prepare the filling blend all the ingredients together in a food processor or high powered blender. Scoop into chilled tart crusts and spread even, smoothing the top with an offset spatula.
4.) Place tarts in the freezer until frozen solid. (2-4 hours) Once frozen all the way through, remove tarts from pans with a knife.
5.) Let thaw for 20 minutes before serving. Top with shredded coconut and a lime wedge.
6.) Store in the freezer.

# RAW Shepard's Pie

**Prep Time: 10 min || Total Time: 10 min**

**Yield: Serves 4**

**Category: Dessert**

**Cuisine: Vegan**

**Ingredients**

- 1 Recipe of RAW Ground Veggie Meat
- 1 Recipe of Cauliflower Smash
- 1 Recipe of Mushroom Gravy
- 1 Recipe of Carrots

**Instructions**

1. Layer the Veggie Meat in the bottom of a small Pyrex dish top with carrots, followed by Cauliflower Smash. Lastly, spread the Mushroom Gravy on the top. Warm in the Dehydrator for 30-40 minutes (Optional).
2. I then topped the serving with some broccoli sprouts that really need to be used up.
3. Also, this did hold up well for one day in the Refrigerator covered.
4. We just warmed it up again for 30-40 minutes to bring it to at least room temperature.

Cauliflower Smash

- 4 cups chopped cauliflower florets
- 1/3 cup of Pine Nuts
- 1 ½ Tablespoon Nutritional Yeast
- 1 clove of Garlic
- ½ teaspoon sea salt
- 1/8 – ¼ teaspoon black pepper

**Instructions**

1. Put all the ingredients into a food processor and mix until achieve a consistency like mashed potatoes.
2. Add more nutritional yeast and seasoning if you want it cheesier. By itself it will keep for 4 days in the fridge

Mushroom Gravy

- 1 cup sliced crimini mushrooms

- ¼ cup of water
- 2 tablespoon chickpea miso (we used white)
- 2 tablespoons olive oil
- 1 tablespoon chopped onion
- 1 teaspoon fresh thyme
- 1 clove garlic
- Dash of Black pepper

## Instructions

1. Process all ingredients in a blender until smooth.
2. Add more water if needed, one tablespoon at a time. Stir before using. By itself it will keep for four days in the refrigerator.

Carrots

- 3 medium carrots shredded
- 2 Tablespoons Olive Oil
- Juice from one Lemon
- Choice of spices – I used the spices I use to use when cooking up ground beef: curry, paprika, chipotle chili pepper and oregano. I didn't measure I just shook.
- Salt and Pepper to taste

## Instructions

1. Mix all the ingredients together in a small ball and let sit for a bit to allow flavors to meld

# Raw Carrot Cake

**Prep Time: 10 min || Total Time: 10 min**

**Category: Dessert**

**Cuisine: Vegan**

**Ingredients**

For the cake

- 1 generous cup walnuts
- 1 generous cup dried unsweetened coconut
- 1 full cup dates, pitted and ground
- 3/4 cup raisins, ground
- 1/4 cup flaxseed, ground fine in coffee grinder
- 5 cups finely ground carrots (grind in food processor until finely ground & juicy)
- 1 teaspoon coriander
- 1/2 teaspoon cardamom

**Instructions**

1. Grind the walnuts in a food processor and leave some in the food processor.
2. Place in a large bowl. Grind dates and raisins in the food processor with the small amount of nuts.
3. Add to bowl with the flaxseed, ground carrots, coriander, and cardamom. Mix by hand, kneading for smoothness.
4. Press the mixture into a spring-form pan or cake pan.

For the frosting

- 2 cups raw cashews, soaked for up to 1 hour
- 2 lemons, juiced
- 2/3 cup raw honey

**Instructions**

Process the cashews, lemon juice, and honey in a food processor until very smooth. Spread on top of the cake mixture in pan.

# Raw Avocado-Pomegranate cake

**Prep Time: 10 min || Total Time: 10 min**

**Category: Dessert**

**Cuisine: Vegan**

**Ingredients**

Base:

- 100g of walnuts
- 100g sunflower seeds
- 65g almonds
- 250g fresh dates
- Cinnamon

**Instructions**

1. Grind the nuts and knead all the ingredients and press into the bottom of the cake pan.

Filling:

- 450g of apples
- 5g dried wheat grass powder
- juice from half lemon
- a little turmeric
- Blend and add 1 avocado. Blend again and add:
- 300g cashew nuts
2. Blend and add:
- 150g of coconut oil if you use it. Otherwise keep your cake in freezer.
3. Blend again.
4. Take few spoons and cool it in the fridge.
5. Prepare seeds from 1 smaller pomegranate.
6. Put pomegranate seeds(half) on the base and pour half of the filling over. Repeat with other half of seeds and filling and freeze. Garnish with pomegranate seeds, ground pistachio and avocado rose.

# Raw Vegan Bagels with Dill & Caper Cashew Cream Cheese

**Prep Time: 10 min || Total Time: 10 min**

**Category: Dessert**

**Cuisine: Vegan**

**Servings: 10**

Raw vegan bagels are one of my current favorite recipes. I love how much like bagels these actually taste, because they have that satisfying slight crunch to the outride of them, with a soft a doughy centre.

## Ingredients

- 1 cup quinoa flour
- 1 cup oat flour
- 1 cup ground almonds
- 2 tbsp psyllium powder
- 1 tbsp onion powder
- 1 tsp garlic powder
- 8 ozs zucchini (courgette) (peeled)
- ¼ cup cashews (soaked 20 mins to 1 hour)
- 2 tablespoons olive oil

- 1 tbsp maple syrup
- ¼ cup nutritional yeast
- 1 tbsp apple cider vinegar
- 1 cup water

Cashew Cream Cheese

- 1 cup cashews (soaked 20 mins to 1 hour)
- ½ cup water
- 1 teaspoon probiotic powder
- 1 tsp salt
- 1 tsp garlic powder
- 2 tsp onion powder
- ¼ cup capers minced
- 2 tbsp fresh dill minced

Assembly

- 1 cup Arugula
- 1/2 cup Baby tomatoes
- 1 Avocado
- 2 tbsp Irish moss gel (optional) (search 'Irish moss gel the raw chef' for method)

## Instructions

Raw Vegan Bagels

1. Mix quinoa flour, oat flour, ground almond, psyllium powder, onion powder, garlic powder together in a large bowl.
2. In a high speed blender, process the zucchini, cashews, olive oil, maple syrup, nutritional yeast, apple cider vinegar and water until smooth and creamy.
3. Add the wet ingredients to the dry and mix well to combine. The mixture will thicken up after about 5 minutes. Once thickened, form into a ball and then roll into bagels, with the use of a mould if you have one. I prefer to make half bagels, so they don't need cutting at a later stage, but you can play around with this.
4. Dehydrate on a nonstick dehydrator tray for 6 to 8 hours at 115 degrees F. Take them off the nonstick sheet and dehydrate for a further 30 minutes to dry the bottoms.
5. Will store in a sealed container for up to 2 weeks.

Cashew Cream Cheese

1. Blend the cashews, water and probiotics in a high speed blender until smooth.
2. Transfer to a bowl, cover and leave in a warm place for 8 to 12 hours to ferment.
3. Once fermented, you'll see the mixture has small air bubbles and tastes slightly sour.
4. Mix in the salt, capers and dill and store in the fridge until ready to serve.
5. Will last up to a week in the fridge.

Assembly

1. Spread some caper dill cream cheese on each bagel half, then add avocado, tomatoes and rocket leaves.
2. I like to also grind some black or white pepper on top. These can be served open faced or as a sandwich.

**Calories: 327kcal, Carbohydrates: 29g, Protein: 10g, Fat: 20g, Saturated Fat: 2g, Sodium: 368mg, Potassium: 368mg, Fiber: 6gSugar: 3gVitamin A: 170IUVitamin C: 8.4mgCalcium: 56mgIron: 2.9mg**

# Low-Fat Banana Walnut Oatmeal

**Prep Time: 10 min || Total Time: 10 min**

**Cuisine: Vegan**

**Makes 3-4 servings**

**Ingredients**

- 1/2 cup walnuts (If you want it to be lower in fat--those doing LFRV*--I'd only add about 1/4 cup walnuts)
- 2-3 bananas
- 2 T ground flaxseed
- 2-3 large soaked dated

**Instructions**

1. Blend in a food processor and enjoy with cut up apples, yum!
2. Feel free to enjoy with homemade coconut milk.

**Calories: 581.3 |Protein: 9.8g | Fat: 23.1g**

# Raw strawberry chocolate cheesecake.

## Ingredients

The recipe for the crust-

- 3/4 cup of pecan nuts
- 3/4 cup of walnuts
- 1/2 cup of dates
- 1/2 tsp of vanilla extract

## Instructions

1. Blend all ingredients together until it combines.
2. I left the nuts a bit choppy for some texture for this one.
3. I layered this on the bottom of a small 12cm spring cake tin, lightly brushed with coconut oil.
4. Stick in the fridge while waiting.

For the middle layer-

- 1/2 cup of cashew nuts (soaked for a minimum of 2 hours)
- 1/2 a cup of strawberries
- 1 + 1/2 TB of raw cacao powder
- 2 TB of pure maple syrup
- 2 TB of coconut oil
- 2 TB of lemon juice

## Instructions

1.  Blend your cashew nuts in your food processor it took me about ten minutes (stopping and starting, to keep the nuts from sticking to the sides) when you get it nice and creamy add the rest of the ingredients and blend until all mixed together.
2.  Get your crust from the fridge and pour your strawberry cream over, and pop into the freezer to set while you make the top layer.

For the top layer-

- 1/2 an avocado
- 2 TB of raw cacao powder
- 2-3 TB of pure maple syrup (depending on how sweet you like it)
- 1/4 cup of mixed walnuts and pecan nuts.
- 2 strawberries + a dash of pure maple syrup (to taste)

**Instructions**

1.  Blend the avocado, raw cacao and maple syrup in your food processor until nice and creamy. Get the cake from the freezer make sure the top is solid enough. Then pour your chocolate cream over and smoothen out with a spatula.
2.  Stick back into the freezer for an hour to make it set. When done have your walnut and pecan mix ready to cover around the cake, I just used a tablespoon and my hands to pat the nuts on.
3.  For the strawberry sauce just blend together the strawberries and maple syrup. Then in diagonal lines, softly pour over the strawberry sauce over the top with a teaspoon.
4.  Ready to eat straight away or keep in the fridge until ready to eat. It's a healthier substitute to a cheese cake and it really does taste amazing.

# Ice cream

## Ingredients

- 1 cup cashews, soaked 1-2 hours
- ½ cup young coconut meat
- ½ cup agave
- 1 ¼ cup water, coconut water, or nut milk
- ¼ cup coconut oil
- 1 tablespoon vanilla extract
- ¼ teaspoon sea salt

## Instructions

1. Blend all ingredients in blender until very smooth. Pour into ice cream machine and freeze according to instructions.

## Fruit carpaccio

Compressed fruit

- 1 apple or pear, stone fruit, or other seasonal fruit, sliced very thin
- 1 tablespoon lemon juice
- 1 teaspoon maple syrup or coconut blossom paste
- pinch cinnamon
- pinch salt

## Instructions

1. In a bowl, whisk together the above ingredients, except the fruit, until well combined. Gently toss
2. together pear or apple or stone fruit slices with the mixture and layer into a bowl to marinade.
3. Alternatively, for a more advanced technique layer in a vacuum sealable bag, taking care not to overlap
4. the pieces over each other. Vacuum seal and store in refrigerator until ready to serve.

## Star anise fruit syrup

## Ingredients

- ½ cup agave*
- 1 tablespoon lemon juice*
- ¼ teaspoon ground star anise
- pinch salt

**Instructions**

1.  Blend or whisk all ingredients until thoroughly combined.

 *For a tropical variation, use 3 tablespoons agave, 3 tablespoons passionfruit juice, and omit lemon juice.

ASSEMBLY

2.  Evenly spread 1-2 small spoonfuls of star anise syrup over the center of a plate.
3.  Gently layer compressed apples or pears flat over the syrup.
4.  Place a quenelle of the vanilla ice cream off center of the dish.\
5.  Garnish with star anise syrup.

# Banana pancakes

## Ingredients

- 1 banana
- 1 cup soaked pecans
- 3⁄4 cup soaked cashews
- 1 tablespoon sifted oat flour (optional)
- 1⁄2 cup maple syrup or agave
- 1⁄4 cup water
- 1⁄2 tablespoon vanilla extract
- 1⁄2 teaspoon salt

## Instructions

1.  Blend ingredients until smooth. Portion pancake batter by 1⁄4 cup onto a non-stick dehydrator sheet, and smooth into pancake rounds.
2.  Dehydrate 24-48 hours. Pancakes can be flipped, but not onto mesh sheet, as they will become imprinted with the mesh texture.
3.  Serve with your choice of toppings, such as fresh fruit, yogurt, and maple syrup.

**Ingredients:** Chocolate chip cookies

- 2 1/2 cups fine cashew flour*
- 1 3/4 cups oat flour, sifted
- 1/2 cup maple syrup**
- 1/4 cup agave or coconut blossom paste
- 1 tablespoon vanilla extract
- 1/2 teaspoon sea salt
- 1 tablespoon dry coconut, palm, or maple sugar (optional)
- pinch cinnamon (optional)
- 1 cup raw chocolate chips* or cacao nibs

*To make cashew flour, blend 1 cup of cashews at a time on high in a high-speed blender. Blending cashews causes them to become soft and buttery very quickly, so be careful to not blend too much at once or to blend on a slow speed.

**1/2 cup maple syrup may be substituted for 1/4 cup maple syrup + 1/4 cup coconut blossom paste or agave

- raw chocolate chips
- 1 cup soaked cashews
- 1/2 cup maple syrup
- 1/2 cup raw cacao powder
- 1/2 teaspoon vanilla extract
- pinch salt

**Instructions**

1. Blend all ingredients except cacao powder until smooth.
2. Place in piping bag and pipe chocolate chips on a non-stick sheet. Dehydrate 24-48 hours at 115 degrees.
3. Keep in the refrigerator until ready to use.

ASSEMBLY

1. Mix all ingredients except chocolate chips in a bowl by hand. Stir in approximately 1 cup of chips to the batter.
2. Form dough into 3 inch cookies and press a few extra chips into the top. Dehydrate overnight at 115 degrees.

# Standard bread

## Ingredients

- 2 cups almond pulp (wet)
- 1/3 cup Irish moss paste or kelp noodle paste
- 1 tablespoon lemon juice
- 3 soft dates
- 1 teaspoon salt
- 1/4 cup oat flour, sifted
- 2 tablespoons flax meal

OPTIONAL FOR GARLIC BREAD

- 1 clove crushed garlic
- 1 teaspoon garlic powder

## Instructions

1. Process Irish moss paste, lemon juice, dates and salt in a food processor until smooth. Add almond pulp and process until well combined.
2. Transfer to a bowl and fold in oat flour and flax, to create your dough.
3. Form into a loaf approximately 1 1/4" high and 2" wide (3cm high and 5 cm wide). Place on a teflex sheet and dehydrate whole loaf for 3 hours.
4. Cut into desired slices and lay out on mesh dehydrator sheet to dehydrate further until desired consistency is achieved.

# Herb Crackers

## Ingredients

- 1 cup almond flour
- 1/4 cup oat or buckwheat flour
- 1/2 teaspoon salt
- 1/4 cup flax meal
- 1 teaspoon fresh thyme
- 1/2 teaspoon fresh rosemary
- 1/2 tablespoon olive oil
- 1/2 cup celery juice

## Instructions

1. Fold all ingredients together until thoroughly combined.
2. Spread batter approximately 1/16 – 1/8-inch-thick on a non-stick dehydrator sheet.
3. Dehydrate at 115oF for 2 hours and then score into 1 x 3 inch rectangles. Return to dehydrator until completely dry.

# Mustard

**Prep Time: 10 min || Total Time: 10 min**

**Yield: 1 cup.**

## Ingredients

- 7 tablespoons whole brown mustard seeds
- 1 1/2 tablespoons whole
- yellow mustard seeds
- 3 tablespoons raw apple cider vinegar
- 3 oz. filtered water
- 1 1/2 tablespoons raw unheated honey
- 1/2 teaspoon
- Celtic sea salt

## Instructions

1. In a pint glass jar put the whole mustard seeds, apple cider, vinegar & water and give it a gentle stir.
2. Cap the jar, but NOT* tightly, and let sit at room temperature for 24 hours.
3. After 24 hours, put the mixture into a blender, add in the honey and Celtic sea salt and blend well. You will have to stop the machine and push down the mustard a couple of times. You might have to add a little more filtered water, but do it a tablespoon at a time, until it becomes a mustard consistency.
4. Store in a glass jar in the refrigerator.

NOTE:

- Make this 3-4 days before using
- If you close it too tightly, some pressure might build up in the
- To make a hotter mustard increase the ratio of yellow mustard seeds.

- To make a milder mustard, increase the brown mustard seeds and decrease the yellow.

# Colorful Zucchini Pasta!

**Yield: 1-2 Servings**

**Prep time: 5-10 minutes**

**Vegan**

**Ingredients:**

- 2-3 small zucchini, spiralized with a spiral slicer
- 1 cup cilantro
- 1 cup chopped, julienned or shredded carrots
- 1 cup diced celery
- 2 tbsp lemon Juice
- 2 tbsp hemp Seeds
- 2 julienned pears
- 2 cups chopped purple Cabbage

**Directions**

1. Toss together and enjoy!

# BREAKFAST

# Enlighten Smoothie Bowl

**Prep Time: 10 min || Total Time: 10 min**

**Yield: Serves 1 - 2 1x**

**Category: Breakfast, Snack, Smoothie**

**Cuisine: Vegan**

**Ingredients**

Top down view of smoothie bowl topped with sliced fruits, nuts, seeds and granola and coconut.

The smoothie bowls of all smoothie bowls! Lots of color, texture and flavor...so delicious!

**Ingredients**

Smoothie mix

- 1 1/2 cups berry mix or frozen fruit mix of choice
- 1 1/2 fresh banana (use the other half sliced on top)
- 2 tablespoons almond or natural peanut butter or 1 scoop vegan protein powder, optional
- 1/2 cup water
- 3 – 4 ice cubes

**Some optional toppings**

Granola, Coconut, Cacao nibs, Natural nut butters (almond, peanut, etc.),
Banana, Blueberries, Strawberries, Grapes, kiwi, Goji berries, Hemp hearts, chia
seeds, pomegranate seeds, almonds, pumpkin seeds

**Instructions**

1.  In blender, place berry mix, banana, nut butter, water and ice cubes.
    Blend until thick and creamy.
2.  Pour into serving dish and top with whatever toppings you like. Serves
    one.

NOTES:

- If using frozen bananas, omit the ice cubes and add 1/4 cup of water.
- Add extra water as needed once blended. If using protein powder you
  may find you need a little extra.
- Adding nuts and seeds as part of your toppings will add extra protein.

Amount Per Serving

**Calories 423, Total Fat 19g 29%, Saturated Fat 1.6g, Cholesterol 0mg
0%, Sodium 6.2mg 0%, Total Carbohydrate 63g21%, Dietary Fiber
12.2g 49%, Sugars 33.6g, Protein 10.1g 20%, Vitamin A0%, Vitamin
C237% Calcium15% Iron14% Vitamin D0% Magnesium 41% Potassium
34%, Zinc 11%, Phosphorus 25%**

# Chewy Superfood Hemp Protein Bars

**Prep Time: 10 min || Total Time: 10 min**

**Category: Breakfast**

**Serves: 12+**

**Ingredients:**

DRY //

- 1 1/2 cup hemp protein powder, chocolate flavor (or original just add more cocoa)
- 1/2 cup hemp hearts, shelled
- 1/2 cup cocoa powder
- 1/2 cup walnuts, ground into a coarse flour
- 1/2 cup pumpkin seeds, whole
- 1/4 cup chia seeds, ground
- 1/4 cup dried mulberries
- 2 tablespoons cacao nibs (optional)
- 2 tablespoons spirulina powder
- 1/4 teaspoon pink himalayan sea salt
- dash of ground cinnamon

WET //

- 1 1/2-2 cups dates, about 20 pitted
- 1/2 cup dried tart cherries
- 5 tablespoons coconut oil, melted
- 1 heaping tablespoon almond butter
- 1/2 cup water (start with 1/4 and add gradually)
- 1 teaspoon vanilla extract

**Instructions**

DRY //

1. Coarsely grind walnuts and chia seeds.
2. Pour into a large mixing bowl and combine all remaining dry ingredients (hemp powder, seeds, cocoa, pumpkin seeds, mulberries, cacao nibs, and seasonings). Set aside.

WET//

1. Combine all wet ingredients in a high speed blender or food processor.

2. This mixture is very thick and sticky so you'll need a powerful kitchen appliance or mix in small batches. Start with 1/4 cup of water in this mixture.
3. Pour wet ingredients into the large mixing bowl with dry ingredients. This is where you can adjust the water and pay close attention to how much you use.
4. Using your hands (the best tools for this!), massage and combine the mixture until everything has come together to form a large ball.
5. If the mixture gets too wet, simply add more cocoa or hemp protein powder. If the mixture isn't wet enough, try adding more coconut oil or a few more dates. The desired texture is a thick, chewy, sticky bar.
6. In an 8×8 or 9×9-inch parchment lined pan, evenly spread the protein bar mixture into the pan.
7. Using your hands and fingertips firmly press the mixture into an even layer until it's even and smooth on top.
8. Chill for at least 2 hours in the fridge.
9. Cut into small pieces or 12 whole bars.
10. Keep some for later in the freezer by wrapping individually in clear wrap or keep in the fridge for later use that week.
11. Enjoy!

# Stuffed Avocados with Crunchy Asian Cabbage Slaw

**Hands-On Time: 20 Mins || Total Time: 20 Mins**

**Category: Breakfast, Snack, Smoothie**

**Yields: 4 servings**

## Ingredients

- 1 cup shredded red cabbage (I recommend using a mandolin)
- 1 cup shredded green cabbage
- 3/4 cup grated carrot (about 1 carrot)
- 1/2 cup shaved red onion
- 4 green onions, thinly sliced
- 1 Tbsp minced fresh ginger
- juice of 1 lime
- 2 Tbsp mirin
- 1 Tbsp rice vinegar
- 1 Tbsp turbinado or brown sugar
- 2 tsp toasted sesame oil
- 2 avocados, halved and pitted
- sesame seeds

## Instructions

4. In a medium bowl, mix together both cabbages, the carrot, red onion, and green onion.
5. In a small bowl, whisk together the ginger, lime juice, mirin, rice vinegar, sugar, and sesame oil. Pour over the cabbage mixture and toss to combine.
6. Carefully scoop a hole in each avocado half. Fill with the slaw and top with sesame seeds. Enjoy!

NOTES

For a smaller appetizer version, top a rice cracker or sesame cracker with a small slice of avocado and a spoonful of slaw. Garnish with sesame seeds.

# Raw Blueberry Coconut Vanilla Cheese Cake

**Prep Time: 1 hr. 10 min || Total Time: 1 hr. 10 min**

**Category: Breakfast, Snack, Smoothie**

**Ingredients**

Crust:

- 1 1/4 cup cashews, soaked and dehydrated
- 3/4 cup rolled oats (Gluten free) soaked and dehydrated
- 1 1/4 cups shredded coconut
- 1/4 tsp himalayan salt
- 1/4 cup raw coconut oil (Extra Virgin)
- 6 Tbsp Water
- 3 Tbsp honey

Blueberry Layer:

- 2 cups organic blueberries
- 4 Medjool dates (pitted)
- 2 Tbsp chia seeds

Vanilla filling:

- 3 cups cashews (soaked 2+ hours)
- 1 cup almond milk
- 1/4 cup lemon juice
- 3/4 cup honey
- 2 vanilla beans (seeds scrapped) or 2 tsp vanilla extract
- 1/4 tsp himalayan salt
- 3/4 cup coconut oil (Extra Virgin)

Preparation:

Crust:

1. Place the cashews, oats coconut and salt in food processor and processed until it reaches a small crumble.
2. Add the coconut oil, water and honey. Process until the batter sticks together. The batter will seem a bit wet, that is alright.
1.) 3.Place the batter in the crust pan and start pressing the dough into the side of the pan, taking it all the way up to the top. Wetting your fingers will help so the batter won't stick to them. Once the sides are done, firmly

and evenly press the batter into the base of the pan. Set aside while you make the filling.

Blueberry Layer:

1. In a food processor, puree the blueberries, chia seeds and dates
2. Pour over crust and dehydrate at 120 degrees for 60 mins
3. Place in the fridge to chill before adding the vanilla filling.

Vanilla Filling:

1. Drain the soaked cashews and place into a blender.
2. Add almond milk, lemon juice honey and vanilla beans/extract. Blend until filling is creamy smooth. If you get any grits, keep blending.
3. With a vortex going, add the coconut oil. Blend long enough to incorporate.
4. Pour the filling over the blueberry layer into the pan. Gently tap the pan on the counter to remove any air bubbles.
5. Add some shredded coconut on top of the filling.
6. Place the finished cheesecake into the freezer to set.
5. Freeze overnight and then move to the fridge.

# V-8

**Prep Time: 10 min || Total Time: 10 min**

**Category: Juice**

**Cuisine: Vegan**

**Makes 3-4 servings.**

It's great to share with non-raw fooders.  Everyone I have given it to has enjoyed it.  The most common comment is that it tastes better than V8.  I found several recipes online and have been working different combinations of the juices until I came up with this.

I use a scale to do this.  1 gram of liquid is 1 milliliter.

33 ml - Spinach Juice

165 ml - Carrot Juice

31 ml - Beat Juice

275 ml - Tomato Juice

140 ml - Red Pepper Juice

34 ml - Onion Juice

159 ml - Celery Juice

6 ml - Garlic Juice (My juicer yields this much from 1 segment of raw garlic)

3/4 tsp sea salt

# Sensational Burrito

**Prep Time: 10 min || Total Time: 10 min**

**Cuisine: Vegan**

**Makes 3-4 servings.**

**Ingredients:**

Burrito Filling:

- Green cabbage
- Purple cabbage
- 1 dried tomato (sun-dried or dehydrated)
- 1 sweet pepper (red, orange, yellow)
- 1 zucchini
- 1/2 head celery
- 1/2 bunch cilantro
- 1/2 tsp cumin
- juice of 1/2 a lime

Topping:

- Diced mango
- Diced tomato

**Instruction**

1. Peel off the outer 1/3 of leaves from the green and purple cabbage. Set them aside to be used as shells.
2. Place the remaining cabbage and filling ingredients into the food processor and create your burrito filling.
3. Toss on your toppings and enjoy this sweet and savory sensation!

# Chocolate Cinnamon Cheesecake with Pecan & Almond Crumble

**Prep Time: 10 min || Total Time: 10 min**

**Category: Dessert**

**Cuisine: Vegan**

**Makes 3-4 servings**

**Ingredient:**

Filling:

- 3c Cashews, soaked
- 1 Lemon, juiced
- 1/2c Raw Cacao Powder
- 1/4c Coconut Oil, liquefied
- 2-3tsp Cinnamon, organic
- 1/4c Sweetener of choice (Agave, Maple, Date Paste, Coconut Sugar, Honey), adjust as needed.
- 1/2tsp Pink Himalayan Salt
- Water as needed

Crust:

- 3/4c Pecans, raw & organic
- 1c Raw Almonds
- Dash of Pink Himalayan Salt
- 1/2tsp Cinnamon
- 1Tbs Coconut Oil, liquefied
- Pinch of ground cloves
- 2Tbs Raw Organic Coconut Flakes
- Handful of Raw Cacao Nibs, maybe 1/4c

Chocolate Drizzle:

- 4 Tbs Coconut Oil, liquefied
- 2 Tbs Raw Cacao Powder
- 1 tsp Cinnamon
- Sweetener of choice (I used agave this time, but usually I use honey, date paste or maple syrup, all are fine

Directions:

Crust:

1. Process all crust ingredients in a Cuisinart until it's a fine texture, it should be a crumble consistency, don't overdo it or will turn in to a dough.

Filling:

2. Blend all ingredients in Vitamix or blender until very smooth and creamy. Add in water as needed.

Drizzle:

Mix ingredients in a small bowl and drizzle on top of cake.

## Instructions

3. Place a 1/2" layer in a 6" spring form pan and press down to create the crust layer.
4. Add in half of the chocolate filling. Spread it out to create a layer.
5. Now take some of the crust and lightly crumble a layer on top of the filling.
6. Add a light layer of raw cacao nibs on top of the crumbled layer.
7. Pour the rest of the filling on top of the crumble layer, being careful not to mix it all up.
8. Add another layer of lightly crumbled crust on top.
9. Set the entire cake in the freezer to set at least one hour.
10. Take it out and drizzle the chocolate on top in any way you fancy.
11. Put back in freezer to harden. Take out after at least 2-3 hours and serve or put in reZuccinni Pasta with an Avocado Basil Pesto (Julia Rose)

# Raw Pasta

**Prep Time: 10 min || Total Time: 10 min**

**Cuisine: Vegan**

**Makes 3-4 servings**

**Ingredients**

- 2 Large Zucchini or 3 medium peeled and spiralised into angel hair

Raw Pasta Sauce - Creamy Basil, lemon and Mint

- 2 cups of fresh basil
- 1 Large avocado or two small (you need over 200gs at minimum)
- 1 Small tomato
- 1 cup of fresh mint
- 1/4 tsp of cumin
- 1/4 tsp of chilli flakes
- juice of one lemon
- Sea salt
- Pepper
- 3 tbsp of water
- 1 clove of garlic crushed

**Instructions**

Combine all ingredients on high in a food processor until well mixed. Taste and season with extra salt or pepper to taste

# Raw Granola with Edible Blossoms

**Prep Time: 10 min || Total Time: 10 min**

**Cuisine: Vegan**

**Makes: 3-4 servings**

## Ingredients

- 4 cups Whole Oats, Soaked overnight or at least 4 hours
- ¾ cup Raw Almonds (I used honey-glazed almonds), chopped
- ¾ cup Raw Walnuts, chopped
- ½ cup Raw Sunflower Seeds
- ¼ cup Raw Pecans, chopped small
- ½ cup Raw Honey (Know your farmer if possible, mine's from a family member in Oregon)
- ¼ cup Agave or Maple (very optional)
- 1 Tbs Cinnamon (or to taste)
- 1 tsp Pink Himalayan Salt

## Directions:

8. Gently blend all ingredients together in a big bowl.
9. Spread on to dehydrator sheets (I didn't use parchment and nothing dripped through).
10. Dry until crunchy/crispy
11. Take out and add more honey and cinnamon to taste, put back in dehydrator until crunchy and done!

12.  I added some edible blossoms from my yard (lavender petals, Bok Choy blossoms, borage, pansies and violas).  You can always add in dried fruit, more nuts, seeds, spices, anything you like.
13.  Top with homemade nut milk, I used hemp milk but all taste good.
14.  Enjoy & Keep Eating Your Plants!

# Strawberry Caramel Tarts

**Prep Time: 10 min || Total Time: 10 min**

**Cuisine: Vegan**

**Makes 3-4 servings**

Raw Recipe Crust

- 1 cup shredded coconut
- ½ cup pecans
- 1 cup walnuts
- 6 Medjool dates (or 12 soaked normal dates)
- 2 tablespoons Agave Syrup
- ¼ teaspoon salt
- 2 tablespoons melted Coconut Oil

Raw Recipe Caramel

- 2 cups of soaked dates – soak for two hours minimum, then drain
- ¼ cup Raw Honey
- 1 tablespoon Almond Butter (you can omit if you can't find it or can't find a raw version. Add 1 more tablespoon of honey instead)
- 2 tablespoons Almond Milk
- ¼ teaspoon salt

Raw Recipe Strawberry Topping

- 500g fresh washed and quartered or halved strawberries
- 2 tablespoons Agave Syrup

## Instructions

8. Soak dates for caramel and base prior to making the raw receipt with suggested times.
9. To make the Raw Crust, combine the nuts in the food processor and blend until finely chopped. Add the rest of the ingredients and blend until a doughy, chunky mix is formed.
10. Press into greased tart tins or you can use muffin tins, or a large cake tin to make one large tart/flan.
11. Cool for 4 hours in the freezer to set prior to filling. DO NOT MISS THIS STEP!
12. Combine all caramel ingredients in a food processor and process until really smooth.
13. Pour into tins, moulds or whatever you are using.  Gently lay all strawberries into your circular layers and add the whole strawberry in the middle for presentation.
14. To get your Agave Syrup really runny, place in a bowl in the sink with warm water about 20 minutes prior to use. Gently pour a dash of agave syrup over each one to get the strawberries shining. Chill for 3 – 6 hrs and then serve.

# Amy's Pea and Cucumber Dip/Spread

**Prepare your sprouted peas**

- 1/2 cup dried peas

**Instructions**

3. Soak overnight in 1 cup water, rinse and drain in the morning and put in a tub in a cupboard.
4. Repeat this the next two days. They should now have little tails.

To the peas add;

- 2-3" diced cucumber
- 1 tsp nutritional yeast
- A couple of fresh sage leaves or some mint
- 2 cloves of garlic
- 1-2 tbsps olive oil

**Instructions**

3. Puree with a hand blender if available or a liquidizer (in this case put cucumber and oil in first)
4. Season with salt and freshly ground black pepper

# Raw Salted Blueberry Chocolate Tart

**Recipe type: Dessert**

**Cuisine: raw vegan**

## Ingredients

For The Crust:

- 70 grams' hazelnut flour
- 75 grams' almond flour
- 2 tablespoons coconut oil
- 2 tablespoons maple syrup
- pinch sea salt

For The Filling:

- 1.5 cups dates, soaked overnight and drained
- ¼ cup cashews
- ¼ cup warm water
- seeds of ½ fresh vanilla bean
- 80 grams 70% dark chocolate, melted

For The Topping:

- 1 cup fresh blueberries
- 30 grams' chocolate, melted
- ½ tsp coconut oil or ghee
- ½ teaspoon coarse sea salt k

**Instructions**

13. In a Cuisinart or blender, combine hazelnut flour, almond flour, coconut oil, maple syrup, and sea salt.
14. Blend to combine.
15. Remove dough from your blender and form into a ball.
16. Press evenly into a tart pan (mine is irregular at 8 inches wide, but you could use two 4.5-inch-wide tart pans).
17. In a blender, combine drained dates, cashews, warm water, vanilla bean, and melted chocolate and blend until creamy in consistency (it took me about 1 minute, total, stopping to scrape down the sides every 15 seconds or so).
18. Spoon out filling over your raw crust.
19. Spread evenly.
20. Top with blueberries, in no particular arrangement.
21. Combine last of the chocolate with coconut oil or ghee, stirring to thoroughly combine.
22. Using a small spoonful at a time, spoon melted chocolate over your berry topping (I used two spoonfuls).
23. Sprinkle coarse salt over.
24. Serve chilled.

# Cinnamon Raspberry Swirl Cheesecake

**Prep Time: 10 min || Total Time: 10 min**

**Cuisine: Vegan**

**Makes 3-4 servings**

Crust Ingredients

- 1/2 cup pecans
- 1/2 cup dates
- 1/4 cup dried coconut flakes
- 1/4 tsp sea salt
- pinch of cinnamon

Base Cheesecake Ingredients

- 2 cups cashews, soaked for 4-6 hours or overnight
- 1/2 cup agave syrup
- 1/4 cup lemon juice
- 1/4 cup water or nut milk
- 2 TB coconut oil
- 1 TB vanilla extract
- 1/2 tsp salt

Raspberry Sauce Ingredients

- 1 cup fresh or frozen raspberries
- 1/4 cup agave syrup
- 1 tsp lemon juice
- 1 tsp vanilla extract
- pinch of salt

## Instructions

1. Combine crust ingredients in either a blender or food small processor until well combined and the consistency of a sticky dough.

2. Spread crust mixture in the bottom of a 6" spring form pan and pat down evenly and firmly. You can get it very flat and even with the smooth bottom of a drinking glass.

3. Blend all base cheesecake ingredients until perfectly smooth and creamy. It should look like a cake batter. You may need to use a tamper if your blender has one.

4. Pour the batter into the spring form pan.

5. Blend the raspberry sauce ingredients together until smooth. You can either mix the sauce into the cheesecake batter or reserve it to spoon on top of the plain cheesecake after it has set.

6. Put the cheesecake into the freezer to firm overnight. Remove it 1-2 hours before you'd like to serve it so it can thaw a bit.

7. Plate with extra raspberries and a light dusting of cinnamon.

Notes

It is very important to soak the cashews for 4-6 hours before using them. This reduces the phytic acid content to make them more digestible and contributes to the smooth and creamy texture of the finished cheesecake. I can't promise that the texture will be the same if you do not soak the nuts!

# Raw Vegan fermented Cranberry Cheesecake with an orange cranberry glaze

This raw cake doesn't just look like a cheesecake; it is one because I made it with fermented nut cheese. DUH! Tastes just like a cheesecake!! Yay.

**Ingredients**

Crust

- 2 cup walnuts (ground)
- 10 dates paste
- 1 tsp vanilla extract or the seeds of a vanilla bean

Filling

- 2 pounds of cultured cashew cream cheese (made with rejuvelac & fermented 2 days)
- 3/4 cup date paste, (or your favorite liquid sweetener)
- 1/2 teaspoon Celtic sea salt
- 1 1/2 Tbsp pure vanilla extract or the seeds from a vanilla bean
- 1/2 cup coconut butter

**Instructions**

1. Blend above ingredients until creamy
2. Stir in a cup of dried cranberries
3. Put aside 1/3 of the filling & add 3/4 cup cranberries & blend for the top layer top with walnuts & a cranberry glaze made with 1/2 cup date paste (or other liquid sweetener) 1/4 cup orange juice & some orange rind, 1/4

cup coconut oil, 3/4 cup cranberries & 1 teaspoon vanilla blended, then add in whole cranberries.

4.  Save some sauce to serve with the cake

# Sweet Potato Pie with Pecan Topping

**Prep Time: 10 min || Total Time: 10 min**

**Cuisine: Vegan**

**Serves 8**

## Ingredients

- 4-5 cups sweet potatoes, peeled and cubed
- 20 medjool dates pitted
- 1 vanilla bean
- 2 teaspoons cinnamon
- 1 teaspoon sea salt
- 2 tablespoons coconut butter
- 3 cups water
- 1 tablespoon psyllium (more if needed for thicker consistency)
- 1 Nut and Date piecrust

Topping:

- 1 cup pecans, chopped
- ¼ cup raw honey

## Instructions

1. Place dates, vanilla, cinnamon, salt, coconut butter, and water in blender and blend until smooth.
2. Add sweet potatoes and blend until very smooth.
3. Add psyllium blending well.
4. Let mixture sit for 5 minutes to thicken.
5. Blend again until smooth.

6.   Place in piecrust and top with chopped pecans sweetened with honey.

# Raw Vegan White Chocolate Macadamia Nut Cookies

**Prep Time: 10 min || Total Time: 10 min**

**Cuisine: Vegan**

**Makes 3-4 servings**

**Ingredients**

- Macadamia Butter* (2 tbsp)
- Coconut Butter* (2 tbsp)
- Rolled Oats (1/2 cup)
- Cacao Butter (1/2 tsp, melted)
- Macadamia Nuts (1/2 cup)
- Walnuts (1/2 cup)
- Honey (1 tbsp, or omit honey and add 2 or 3 more dates)
- Dates (3-4, pitted)
- Vanilla Powder (1/8 tsp, optional)

**Instructions**

1. Pulse oats in a food processor until ground fine, about 10 seconds.
2. Add the nut butters, honey, dates, a pinch of vanilla powder, and your melted cacao butter to the food processor and let it run until combined.
3. The cacao butter is what will give it that subtle white chocolate flavor, it's actually used as the base of white chocolate.
4. Add walnuts, now add your slightly crushed macadamia nuts. And yes, they are slightly crushed because you just did that by whatever means necessary.
5. Shape them into cookies.

**Note**

- You can store these in the fridge for a while or freeze them for a scary long time. I'd go with 2 weeks in the fridge and a month frozen. They won't last that long either place. Enjoy!
- You can make the butters yourself using a high powered blender. For coconut butter use a high quality shredded coconut and let it blend for a few minutes.

# Raw Vegan Pumpkin Pie

**Prep Time: 10 min || Total Time: 10 min**

**Cuisine: Vegan**

**Makes 3-4 servings**

## Ingredients

Crust

- 1 cup ground macadamia nuts
- 1/3 cup finely grated coconut flakes
- 9 soft medjool dates
- a pinch of sea salt
- 1 teaspoon vanilla

## Instruction

1. Put in a food processor until all ingredients are well mixed, then press around the pie pan to form your crust

Pumpkin filling

- 2 1/2 cups truly raw cashews (soaked)
- 1 cup fresh raw pumpkin puree' (drained in a sieve)
- 1/2 cup liquid sweetener of your choice
- 1 tablespoon vanilla
- 2 teaspoons cinnamon
- 1/2 teaspoon ginger
- 1/8 teaspoon cloves
- 1/8 teaspoon nutmeg
- 1/4 teaspoon sea salt

## Instructions

2. Mix ingredients in a blender until creamy, then pour over the crust & fill the pie pan.
3. Place in the freezer long enough to firm up.

# Raw Creamy Chocolate Cake

**Prep Time: 10 min || Total Time: 10 min**

**Cuisine: Vegan**

**Makes 1-2 servings**

**Ingredients**

BASE:

- 1 and half C walnuts
- 1/2 C almonds
- 4 Tbs cacao
- 8 to 10 soaked medjool dates
- 1Tbs coconut oil
- a sprinkle sea salt

Instructions

- Blend nuts and transfer to bowl.
- Blend remaining then stir both together.
- Press in 20cm pan.


FILLING:

- 350g soaked raw cashews
- 2 whole peeled oranges
- 6 soaked dates
- 50g raw cacao
- 3/4 cup coconut oil
- a sprinkle sea salt.

**Instructions**

1. Blend everything together except coconut oil till smooth.
2. Then add oil, further blend and pour over base. Chill over night

# Caramel dipping sauce

**Prep Time: 10 min || Total Time: 10 min**

**Makes: 3-4 servings**

Can be served with apples, but you will also like it on pears!!

Here is an easy raw treat that kids will love for Halloween (or any day)

## Ingredients

Caramel

- 10 soft medjool dates
- 1/4 cup water
- 1/4 cup liquid sweetener of your choice
- 3 tablespoons coconut butter
- 1 1/2 teaspoons vanilla extract or a whole vanilla bean
- a pinch of sea salt

## Instructions

1. Blend until creamy.

# Sprouted Green Pea Hummus

**Prep Time: 10 min || Total Time: 10 min**

**Cuisine: Vegan**

### Ingredients:

- 2 1/2 - 3 cups sprouted peas
- 1 avocado
- The juice of 1 lemon
- 1/2 cup of tahini
- 2 large cloves of garlic
- 1/4 cup olive oil (optional)
- sea salt & fresh cracked pepper to taste

### Instructions

1. Mix in a blender. Top with chopped red onion, chipotle & pumpkin seeds.
2. Serve with raw crackers or crudité platter

# Barbecue Sauce

**Prep Time: 10 min || Total Time: 10 min**

**Cuisine: Vegan**

**Makes 3-4 servings**

## Ingredients:

- 1/2 cup sun dried tomatoes
- 3/4 cup water
- 5 medjool dates
- 1 pineapple slice
- 2 tablespoons raw apple cider vinegar
- 1 tablespoon cold pressed extra virgin olive oil
- 2 cloves of garlic
- 1 tablespoon onion powder or fresh onion
- 1 tablespoon raw spicy mustard
- 1 teaspoon Celtic sea salt
- 1/2 teaspoon fresh cracked pepper
- 1/4 - 1/2 teaspoon chipotle (depending on how spicey you like it)

## Instructions

1.  Mix above ingredients in the blender, then brush the sauce on your veggies & eat or dehydrate for a few hours to soften the veggies a little

# Onion Bhaji.

**Prep Time: 10 min || Total Time: 10 min**

**Cuisine: Vegan**

**Makes 3-4 servings**

## Ingredients

- 4 red onions - thinly sliced
- 1 cup sunflower seeds - soaked overnight and drained
- 2 sun dried toms and 1 date - soaked overnight
- 2 tbsp cold pressed olive oil
- 1 tbsp sherry vinegar
- 1 tbsp rice wine vinegar
- 1 clove garlic
- Bunch coriander/cilantro - chopped
- 1 red chilli (leave seeds in for very hot)
- 1 tsp ground cumin
- 1tsp ground coriander
- water to make batter

## Instructions

1. Put all ingredients in a blender (incl soak water from tomato/dates) EXCEPT onions. Add water as necessary to make a thick batter/paste.
2. Stir in the onions. Spoon onto dehydrator sheets and dehydrate overnight.
3. Don't be put off by taste of batter or half dehydrated bhaji. They are PERFECT when done

# Pizza crust - the Russel James recipe.

**Prep Time: 10 min || Total Time: 10 min**

**Cuisine: Vegan**

**Makes 3-4 servings**

## Ingredients

- 3 cups sprouted buckwheat
- 2 avocados or 1/2 cup almond butter
- 1/4 cup olive oil
- 1/4 cup fresh basil
- 3 tablespoons Italian seasoning
- 1/2 cup sun-dried tomatoes
- 3 tablespoons lemon juice
- 1/2 teaspoon salt
- 3 medium tomatoes

## Instructions

1. Grind all ingredients in a food processor until they have a paste consistency.

2.  Spread approximately 1/2" thick onto a Paraflex sheet in a circle and dehydrate at 115° F for a few hours, or until you are able to turn it upside down onto another dehydrator tray and peel off the nonstick Paraflex sheet.
3.  Dehydrate for another 8 to 10 hours or until base is dry enough to hold together.

# Rye Crackers

**Prep Time: 10 min || Total Time: 10 min**

**Cuisine: Vegan**

**Makes 3-4 servings**

## Ingredients

- 1 cup ground flax
- 1/2 cup flax seeds
- 1/4 cup sesame seeds
- 1 Tbsp psyllium husks
- 1 Tbsp caraway seeds
- pinch of salt

1. Mix in a large bowl ---

- 1/4 cup buckwheat
- 1 cup chopped carrots (2 med size)
- (or 1 carrot and 1/2 med zucchini)
- 2 Tbsp lemon juice
- 2 Tbsp tamari

- 1 Tbsp dried onion bits
- 1/2 Tbsp dried garlic bits
- 3 cups water

**Instructions**

2. Blend until smooth ---
3. Pour blended mix into large bowl and stir well.
4. Stir every five minutes for 30-45 minutes.
5. divide in half and spread out onto a non-stick Tflex sheet
6. score out your shape
7. Dehydrate at 115F for 24 - 36 hours - flipping part way through.
8. Store in an airtight container. These can be frozen as well.

# Eggplant turn overs

**Prep Time: 10 min || Total Time: 10 min**

**Cuisine: Vegan**

**Makes 3-4 servings**

**Ingredient**

Marinade

- 1 tsp maple syrup
- 2 Tbsp oil
- 2 Tbsp tamari
- 1/4 cup water

**Instructions**

1. Stir and reserve 1-2 Tbsp for the filling

Eggplant

2. Peel the eggplant
3. Slice 1/4" thick or slightly less
4. Use a shallow dish
5. Sprinkle salt and brush marinade on the bottom of the dish.
6. Layer with eggplant
7. Sprinkle salt and bruch marinade on top.
8. Repeat layer by layer.
9. Set it aside

The filling

- 1/2 cup walnuts
- 2 cups rough chopped mushrooms
- 1 Med size fresh tomato
- 1/4 cup fresh parsley
- 1/4 cup sun dried tomato (soak/soft)
- 2 Tbsp diced celery (about half a stalk)
- 2 Tbsp minced red onion
- 1 fresh sage leaf
- 1 small sprig rosemary
- 1 garlic clove
- 3 oregano leaves
- 1/4 tsp nutmeg

- 1-2 Tbsp of the marinade

**Instructions**

1. Process in a food processor until small bits, almost a paste but you can leave some texture ---
2. Put into a bowl and set aside

The sauce

- 2 med size tomatoes
- 1 soft date
- 1/4 cup sun dried tomatoes (soak/soft)
- 1 garlic clove
- salt

**Instructions**

1. Process into a sauce leaving some chunks for texture
2. Pulse in 2 handfuls of baby spinach
3. Pulse in 2 Tbsp diced red onion - or 2 green onions sliced thin.
4. The eggplant rounds will be soft and supple by now.
5. Place a small amount of the filling in the center of an eggplant round, fold over to create the half-moon. Press down in the edges with your fingers.
6. Transfer to a non-stick dehydrator sheet.
7. Spoon sauce over, smooth and press a little with the back of the spoon, to cover the entire eggplant half-moon. Sauce should stay on there easily.
8. Dehydrate at 115F approximately 4 hours. The longer you leave them in the crispier they will get.

# Raw Vegan Pizza: Pesto & Caramelized Onion

**Prep Time: 10 min || Total Time: 10 min**

**Cuisine: Vegan**

**Makes 3-4 servings**

## INGREDIENTS

Base

- 3 cups buckwheat sprouted
- 2 avocados or 1/2 cup almond butter
- 1/4 cup olive oil
- 1/4 cup fresh basil
- 3 tbsp Italian seasoning
- 1/2 cup sun-dried tomatoes
- 3 tbsp lemon juice
- 1/2 tsp salt
- 3 tomatoes medium size

CARAMELIZED ONIONS

- 1 cup soft dates
- 3 tbsp tamari
- 2 tbsp olive oil

- 1/4 cup water
- 5 onions large, sliced thinly (Use a mandoline if you have one)

## PESTO

- 2 cups basil
- 1/4 cup pine nuts
- 1 tbsp olive oil
- 1/4 tsp salt
- 2 tsp lemon juice

## TOMATO SAUCE

- 10 basil leaves
- 1 cup sun-dried tomatoes
- 1 cup tomatoes
- 2 tsp lemon juice
- 1/4 onion medium size
- 1 soft date

## CHEESE

- 1 cup macadamias
- 1 1/2 tbsp lemon juice
- 1/4 tsp salt
- 1/4 cup water
- 1 tbsp nutritional yeast

## INSTRUCTIONS

### BASE

1. Grind all ingredients in a food processor until they have a paste consistency.
2. Spread approximately 1/2″ thick onto a Paraflexx sheet in a circle and dehydrate at 115° F for a few hours, or until you are able to turn it upside down onto another dehydrator tray and peel off the nonstick Paraflexx sheet.
3. Dehydrate for another 8 to 10 hours or until base is dry enough to hold together.

### CARAMELIZED ONIONS

4. Blend all ingredients except the onions in a high-speed blender, until smooth.
5. In a bowl, hand mix the date mixture with the onions until they are thoroughly covered.

6.  Dehydrate at 115° F on a non-stick sheet for 2 to 3 hours, so they soften and take on a cooked appearance.

## PESTO

7.  Pulse all ingredients in a food processor until broken down, but leave some texture to the finished pesto.

## TOMATO SAUCE

8.  Blend all ingredients in a high-power blender until smooth.

## CHEESE

9.  Grind all ingredients in a food processor until they have a fluffy consistency.

## ASSEMBLY

10.  Spread the tomato sauce onto the base.
11.  Then sprinkle on the pesto, macadamia cheese and caramelized onions evenly to produce a beautiful layered and textured pizza.

# SMOOTHIES AND DRINKS

# Mixed Berry Smoothie Bowls

**Prep Time10 minutes || Total Time10 minutes**

**Servings: 2 small smoothie bowls**

**Vegan**

This thick smoothie bowl is filled with berry flavor!

## Ingredients

- 2 bananas frozen
- 3/4 cup mixed berries frozen
- 1/2 cup plain yogurt dairy-free if needed
- 1/4-1/2 cup carrot orange juice use less for a thicker smoothie
- 1 handful cauliflower
- 1 tablespoon flaxseed

## Instructions

1. Blend all ingredients together until smooth and enjoy!

# Raw creamy Pasilla Chile soup dressing or smoothie

**Prep Time: 10 min || Total Time: 10 min**

**Category: Smoothie or dressing**

**Cuisine: Vegan**

**Ingredients**

- 1/2 c sunflower seeds
- 1/4 c peanut milk
- 2 dried pasilla peppers
- 2 cloves of garlic
- 1 whole tomato
- A generous pinch of sun dried tomatoes
- Half a lemon
- Half a cucumber
- Generous t of sea salt
- 3/4 c water

**Instructions**

1. Blend and eat as a dressing on your salad, a sauce over your zucchini, or drink as a smoothie.

# Mango Mint CBD Lemonade

**Vegan**

**Ingredients**

- 1 ripe mango, peeled, pit removed, and cubed
- 2 tbsp chopped mint
- 6 tbsp water
- 3 organic lemons (juiced)
- 0.5 cup organic cane sugar
- 5 cups cold water
- CBD Oil or CBD Isolate Powder

**Instructions**

1. Add Mango and 6 tablespoons of water to a food processor or small blender
2. Blend until smooth
3. Pour the mango into a large pitcher
4. Add the lemon juice and sugar to pitcher and stir until combined
5. Add 5 cups of cold water and stir
6. Pour over ice in your favorite glass
7. Add your desired dose of CBD Oil or Isolate Powder, then stir.
8. Kick back, relax, and enjoy

# Pumpkin Pie Juice

**Prep Time: 10 min || Total Time: 10 min**

**Category: Juice**

**Cuisine: Vegan**

**Ingredients:**

- 2 cups of pumpkin
- 2 large carrots
- 2 apples
- 1 pear
- 1" piece of ginger (or to taste)

**Instructions**

1.) Peel pumpkin.
2.) Wash produce and chop to size to fit through your juicer.
3.) Juice and enjoy!

**Substitutions:**

- Pumpkin – sweet potato, butternut squash (butternut pumpkin)
- Carrot – sweet potato, beets (beetroots)
- Apples – pear, orange, mandarin
- Pear – apple
- Ginger – nutmeg, cinnamon

# Green Superfood and Almond Smoothie Bowl

**Prep Time: 10 min || Total Time: 10 min**

**Category: Juice**

**Cuisine: Smoothie**

You won't taste the kale or spinach in this superfood smoothie bowl, but those deep greens give this recipe a major nutritional upgrade while raw almonds and chia seeds pack in some excellent plant-based protein.

**Ingredients:**

Makes one smoothie bowl.

Smoothie:

- 1 raw medium banana
- ½ cup fresh kale
- ½ cup fresh spinach
- ½ cup water
- 1 tbsp. raw almonds

Toppings:

- ½ medium banana, sliced
- 1 tbsp. chia seeds
- 1 tbsp. smooth raw almond butter

**Instructions:**

1. Add the smoothie ingredients to a blender, and blend thoroughly until very smooth. Add more water if you desire a more liquid texture.
2. Pour green smoothie into a serving bowl.
3. Add toppings in a row on the surface of the smoothie, including banana slices, chia and almond butter in that order.
4. Serve fresh.

# Cacao Maca drink powder

**Prep Time: 10 min || Total Time: 10 min**

**Category: Juice**

**Cuisine: Vegan**

**Ingredients**

- 1/4 cup hemp hearts
- 1 Tbsp raw date sugar
- 2 Tsp lucuma powder
- 1 TBSP maca powder
- 2 Tbsp Cacao powder
- pinch of salt

**Instructions**

1. Mix all ingredients together.
2. Store in an air tight jar, fridge or cool cupboard.
3. Use 2 Tbsp per 8oz of water.
4. Plus 1 Fat Cube if you want the full fat version.
5. Blend until warm.

# Raw Vegan Chocolate Ice Cream

## Ingredients:

- 3 cups almond milk
- 4 cups cashews (soaked)
- 3/4 cup liquid sweetener (date paste, honey, raw agave, maple syrup, etc.)
- slightly less than1/2 cup raw cacao powder
- 2 vanilla beans
- 1 tablespoon lacuma powder
- a pinch of sea salt

## Instructions

Mix all ingredients in your blender, run process in an ice cream maker. (you can skip this step, bit the ice cream might get a little hard in the freezer & need to be thawed slightly before serving.

# Matcha Moringa Latte

## Ingredients

- 1 tsp matcha powder
- 1 tsp moringa powder
- 1-2 Tbsp hemp hearts
- 1 Tbsp coconut milk powder
- 1 tsp vanilla powder or extract
- 1-2 dates, date sugar or sweetener of your choice
- 1 Tbsp coconut oil (optional)
- 8 oz. of water

## Instructions

1. Blend until warm
2. Dust with cinnamon

# SIDE, SALAD AND DRESSING

# Creamy Raw Vegan Tzatziki

**Prep Time: 10 minutes || Total Time: 10 minutes**

**Course: Side Dish, Snack**

**Servings: 8 servings**

Creamy raw vegan tzatziki that's completely nut-free and oil-free. Packed with

fresh herbs and tons of favor, this is a must try! Perfect on Portobello Gyros or as a spread.

## Ingredients

- 1 cup hemp seeds
- 2- 3 cloves garlic minced
- juice of two lemons
- 2 tablespoons heaping tahini
- 2-3 persian cucumbers or 1 large
- 1 tablespoon chopped fresh mint
- 1 tablespoon chopped fresh parsley
- 1 tablespoon chopped fresh dill
- 4 tablespoons water

## Instructions

1. Chop the cucumbers into small pieces. In a blend or food processor, combine the hemp seeds, tahini, minced garlic, lemon juice, and water.
2. Blend or process until smooth and creamy. If it's too thick, add water 1 tablespoon at a time until you reach your desired consistency.
3. Transfer to a medium bowl. Stir in the herbs and chopped cucumber. Serve immediately or keep refrigerated in an airtight container for 2-3 days.

# Raw Vegan Curried Cabbage Salad

**Total: 10 mins || Prep: 10 mins**

**Cook: 0 mins**

**Yield: 4 servings**

## Ingredients

- 1 head green cabbage (chopped)
- 1/3 cup shredded flaked coconut (be sure it's raw if needed)
- 2 tbsp lemon juice
- 1/4 cup cold-pressed olive oil
- 1/4 cup soy sauce (if raw, use nama shoyu)
- 3 tbsp sesame seeds
- 1/3 tsp turmeric
- 1/2 tsp curry
- 1/2 tsp cumin

## Instructions

1. In a large bowl, toss together all ingredients, making sure cabbage is evenly coated.
2. If possible, chill for at least an hour and toss thoroughly again before serving. This will allow all the flavors to mingle and blend.

Nutritional Guidelines (per serving)

**Calories: 272, Fat: 19g, Carbs: 23g, Protein: 7g**

# Raw Peanut Zoodle Salad

**Prep Time: 10 Minutes || Total Time: 10 Minutes**

**Yield: 5 Servings**

**Vegan**

15 minute Raw Peanut Zoodle Salad with spiralized zucchini, shredded carrots and a simple peanut dressing.

**Ingredients**

PEANUT DRESSING

- 2 tablespoons | 30 ml sesame oil
- 1/2 cup | 125 g peanut butter (can use tahini for a peanut free option)
- 1 tablespoon fresh ginger, minced
- 2 tablespoons coconut sugar
- 3 tablespoons | 45 ml tamari or coconut aminos
- 1 tablespoon | 15 ml rice vinegar
- 1/2 teaspoon freshly ground black pepper + more to taste

SALAD

- 2 large zucchinis, spiralized into spaghetti-like noodles
- 1 large carrot
- 2 tablespoons fresh cilantro, chopped
- 1/2 cup chopped green onions
- 1/4 cup raw, un roasted peanuts, chopped
- 1 tablespoon | 15 ml tabasco sauce (optional)

**Instructions**

1. In a small mixing bowl whisk together the sesame oil, peanut butter, sugar, tamari/coconut aminos, ginger, vinegar and pepper. Set aside.
2. Use a grater and shred the carrots.
3. Add the zucchini and carrot to a large bowl. Add the sauce and toss everything together. Sprinkle over the cilantro, green onions, peanuts and tabasco sauce and serve immediately.

NOTES

1. If you use coconut aminos you will need to increase the amount of salt you use. Season to your taste preference.
2. Make it paleo: Use cashews instead of peanuts, almond butter in place of peanut butter and coconut aminos instead of soy/tamari.

**Amount Per Serving: Calories: 290 Saturated Fat: 4g Sodium: 451mg Carbohydrates: 17g Fiber: 3g Sugar: 8g Protein: 9g**

# Raw Beet and Sweet Potato Salad

**Prep time: 10 Minutes || Total time: 10 Minutes**

**Course: Side Dish**

**Servings: 6**

Amazing fresh Raw Beet and Sweet Potato Salad with scallions, pepitas, and garlic lime dressing. This is not your average beet salad!

## Ingredients

- 2 large sweet potatoes
- 1 bunch beets 3-4
- 4 scallions
- 1/2 cup toasted pepitas pumpkins seeds
- Garlic Lime Vinaigrette

## Instructions

1. Peel the sweet potatoes and beets. Then use a spiralizer to cut the veggies into long curly strips.
2. Use a pair of kitchen shears to cut the pieces into manageable lengths.
3. Mix the beet and sweet potato ribbons together in a large bowl. Then cut the scallion tops on an angle to make long rings.
4. Sprinkle the salad with scallions and pepitas. Serve with your favorite vinaigrette.

**Serving: 1cup, calories: 169kcal, carbohydrates: 11g, protein: 2g, fat: 13g, saturated fat: 2g, cholesterol: 0mg, sodium: 36mg, potassium: 255mg, fiber: 2g, sugar: 3g, vitamin a: 6225iu, vitamin c: 3.2mg, calcium: 23mg, iron: 1mg**

# Raw Vegan Tacos

**Vegan**

For a raw vegan taste of Mexico, give this delicious taco recipe a try! It features a blend of classic Mexican vegetables, salad fruits and spicy salsa atop fresh and crispy Romaine lettuce leaves.

**Ingredients:**

- 4 leaves of Romaine lettuce
- 1/2 small lime

Raw Tomato Salsa: (Makes around 2 cups)

- 1.5 cups finely chopped tomatoes
- 1/4 cup finely chopped green bell pepper
- 1 small onion, finely chopped
- 2 tsp chopped raw jalapeno pepper (with seeds)
- 1/8 cup finely chopped fresh cilantro
- 1/4 teaspoon ground cumin
- 1 tbsp fresh lime juice
- Dash of sea salt
- Freshly ground black pepper to taste

Raw Taco Filling:

- 1 cob of sweet corn
- 1 small avocado, chopped
- 1 small tomato, chopped
- 2 small baby sweet peppers, chopped
- 1/2 stalk celery, chopped finely
- 1 tbsp hemp hearts
- Salt, pepper and lime juice to taste.

**Instructions:**

1. Prepare salsa by mixing ingredients in a bowl or gently grinding in a molcajete. Store 1.75 cups for later, and set the remaining 1/4 cup aside for this recipe. Makes around 2 cups.
2. Cut corn off cob and place in bowl.
3. Add the other taco filling ingredients and a tablespoon of salsa to the bowl. Massage with hands to mix the ingredients and mash the avocado chunks.

4.  Place the Romaine leaves together on a serving plate in a desirable pattern.
5.  Spoon taco filling carefully into the lettuce leaves along the spine. Take any extra filling and place at the base of the leaves.
6.  Take the salsa that was set aside, and drip it along each of the tacos and on top of the extra filling.
7.  Serve fresh.

Enjoy

# Raw creamy almond orange ginger salad dressing

## Ingredients

- 3/4 cup raw almonds
- 2 large navel oranges
- 1 cup water
- 1-inch knob fresh ginger
- 1/4 cup balsamic vinegar
- 1 Tbsp miso paste
- Black pepper to taste

## Instructions

1. Blitz it all in the high speed blender and use on veggies, salads, sandwiches.

# Asian Zucchini Noodle Salad Recipe

**Prep time: 20 minutes || Yield: Serves 4**

Some vegetables can be harder to digest when they are raw, like cauliflower or zucchini. So, if you are not used to eating raw zucchini, take it easy the first time, and don't eat more than a regular portion.

## Ingredients

- 3 to 4 zucchinis (1 1/2 pounds total)
- 1/2 teaspoon salt
- 1 1/2 cups thinly sliced and roughly chopped red cabbage
- 1 large carrot, grated (about 1 cup)
- 1/2 large red bell pepper, thinly sliced then cut into 1-inch segments
- 2 green onions, thinly sliced on the diagonal
- 1/2 bunch cilantro, chopped, leaves and tender stems (about 1/2 cup)

Dressing:

- 1/3 cup seasoned rice vinegar*
- 2 tablespoons extra virgin olive oil
- 1 1/2 teaspoons dark roasted sesame oil
- 1 clove garlic, minced (about 1 teaspoon)
- Pinch of red pepper flakes

***Seasoned rice vinegar** is rice vinegar that has been seasoned with salt, pepper, and sugar. If you have plain rice vinegar, you'll need to add seasoning and sugar to it.

## Instructions

1. **Spiralize zucchini noodles:** Using a spiralizer or other spiral vegetable slicing tool, use the zucchini to make the zucchini noodles following manufacturer's directions. You should have 5 to 6 cups of "zoodles".
2. Place in a colander set over a bowl and toss with salt. Let the noodles drain a bit of their excess moisture while you prep the other vegetables.
3. Many of the noodles are quite long, so you'll want to cut them up a bit with scissors to make them easier to toss with the other vegetables.
4. **Combine zucchini noodles** with cabbage, carrot, bell pepper, onions, cilantro in a large bowl.
5. **Make dressing:** Whisk together in a medium bowl the seasoned rice vinegar, olive oil, dark sesame oil, minced garlic, and red pepper flakes.

6.  Pour the dressing over the zucchini noodles and vegetables and gently toss to combine.
7.  Serve immediately

# Oil-Free Green Goddess Dressing

**(Vegan)**

**Prep time: 10 mins || Total time: 10 mins**

**Serves: 1½ cups**

Using the ingredients listed on Annie's bottled dressing as my guide, the resulting dressing recipe is downright delicious, and much healthier than the original!

**Ingredients**

- ½ cup raw tahini
- ½ cup water
- 2 Tablespoons fresh parsley, chopped
- 2 Tablespoons green onions, chopped
- ½ teaspoon sea salt
- 3 cloves garlic (or 1½ tsp. garlic powder)
- 1 teaspoon Nama Shoyu or Tamari
- 2 Tablespoons fresh lemon juice
- 2 Tablespoons raw Apple Cider Vinegar

Instructions

1. Combine all of the ingredients into a blender or food processor, and blend until smooth and creamy.
2. Adjust seasoning to taste, and add more water, if necessary, until desired texture is achieved.
3. Serve immediately, or store in the fridge for up to 4 days in a sealed container. This dressing will thicken up when chilled, making a nice veggie dip or creamy sauce for spiralized noodles, too!

Notes

Note: For those who must avoid vinegar, feel free to substitute extra lemon juice instead, and choose tamari (wheat-free soy sauce) if you're gluten-sensitive.

# SOUP

# Blueberry Lavender Latte

**Prep Time: 15 minutes || Soak Time: 2 hours**

**Total Time: 2 hours 15 minutes**

**Servings: 4**

**Vegan**

Enjoy this beverage hot or cold with cashew milk, blueberries, and lavender.

## Ingredients

- 1/2 cup raw cashews soaked for 2 hours
- 2 cups filtered water
- 3/4 cup blueberries fresh or frozen
- 3 dates pitted
- 2 teaspoons dried lavender buds food grade
- 1 pinch sea salt
- 1 splash vanilla extract optional

## Instructions

1. Soak cashews in a dish with warm water (enough to cover), 1/8 teaspoon salt, and 1/4 teaspoon apple cider vinegar.
2. Loosely cover the dish with a towel and let soak for 2 hours. Drain soaking liquid and rinse well.
3. Blend soaked cashews, water, blueberries, pitted dates, vanilla, and sea salt in a blender until smooth (30+ seconds).
4. Heat cashew blueberry milk in a saucepan on the stovetop or in a microwave-safe container in the microwave.
5. Using a tea infuser, steep lavender buds in the mixture for 5 – 10 minutes.
6. Enjoy warm or chilled over ice.

# Roasted" Tomato Basil Soup

**Prep time: 20 mins || Total time: 20 mins**

**Vegan**

**Type: Main dish, appetizer**

**Serves: 2**

## Ingredients

Soup

- 4 large tomatoes, chopped
- 1/4 mild onion, chopped
- 2 tablespoons olive oil
- 1 tablespoon dried oregano
- 1 tablespoon dried basil
- pinch salt and pepper
- 2 cups water
- 1/2 cup Brazil nut milk (See notes below)

## Instructions

1. You will need to dehydrate the tomatoes for 6 hours.

2. You can soak the Brazil nuts at the same time for the nut milk.
3. In a large bowl, combine chopped tomatoes, onion, oil, basil, oregano, salt and pepper. Let sit for 1/2 hour. Drain.
4. Place tomatoes on teflex sheets and dehydrate for 1/2 hour at 146 degrees and then 5.5 hours @ 116 degrees.
5. Place tomatoes, onions and 2 cups water in the Vitamix Puree.
6. Add 1/2 cup Brazil nut milk, quickly blend.
7. You can lightly heat the soup in your dehydrator.

## Brazil Nut Milk (4 cups)

- 1 cup Brazil nuts
- 4 cups water

## Instructions

1. Soak the nuts in the water for 6 hours.
2. Place in vitamix. Process until very well blended.
3. Strain through cheese cloth or nutmilk bag.

# Raw Spicy Mango Ginger Soup

**Total: 10 mins ||Prep: 10 mins**

**Yield: 2 servings**

**Vegan**

All of the ingredients in this recipe for spicy mango soup are fresh and healthy. This cold soup recipe is suitable for those on a gluten-free diet or a raw food diet, as it is vegetarian, vegan and uses all fresh, raw food ingredients. And it's fat-free and gluten-free too!

Spicy chilies pair well fresh mangoes, and with a bit of ginger for an extra kick, this is a cold soup recipe to keep!

**Ingredients**

- 1 large mango (peeled and destoned)
- 1/2 onion (chopped)
- 1/2 cup cold water
- 1 to 2 small chili peppers (minced)
- Juice from 1 lime
- 1/2 tsp. ginger (grated or minced)

**Instructions**

1. Process all ingredients together in a blender until smooth and creamy, adding a bit more or less water as needed.
2. Chill before serving.

# Vital Green Soup

**Vegan**

I made this soup for the first time today. I came up with the recipe myself it's packed with nutrition; I am aware it's low on proteins recipe will be updated.

## Ingredients

- 4 oz. of Kambucha
- 3/4 cup Papaya
- 1/2 Cucumber
- 1/2 Carrot
- 3 Baby bella mushrooms
- 1/2 cup Watercress
- 6 Green beans
- 1 Celery heart
- 1/2 cup Salanova lettuce
- Pinch of Alfalfa sprouts
- Pinch of Rosemary
- Pinch of Oregano
- Pinch of green onion
- 1 turmeric root
- 1tsp of ground pepper to boost turmeric effects
- Dulse

## Instructions

1.  Blend little by little to avoid blender getting warm and ingredients cooking themselves

# Avocado Lime Soup

**Ingredients**

- 2 avocados
- 3/4 of a medium cucumber
- 1 stalk celery
- Juice of 1 lime
- Small handful of fresh coriander
- 2 teaspoons cumin
- 1 teaspoon ground coriander
- 1/2 teaspoon salt
- 1 teaspoon coconut aminos
- 1 cup water

Instructions

1.  Blend all ingredients, except the sour cream and chopped chives, in a high-speed blender until smooth.

Sour cream

- 1 1/2 cups cashews
- 2 tablespoons lemon juice
- 1 tablespoon + 1 teaspoon apple cider vinegar
- 1 cup water
- 1/2 teaspoon salt

Instruction

1. Blend all ingredients in a high-speed blender.
2. Add a little extra water one tablespoon at a time if you're having trouble getting the cashews smooth.